SOUTHERN
FARMERS MARKET
COOKBOOK

Collard
GREENS
picked yesturday!

SOUTHERN
FARMERS MARKET
COOKBOOK

HOLLY HERRICK

PHOTOGRAPHS BY RICK McKEE

GIBBS SMITH
TO ENRICH AND INSPIRE HUMANKIND

Salt Lake City | Charleston | Santa Fe | Santa Barbara

First Edition
13 12 11 10 09   5 4 3 2 1

Published by
Gibbs Smith
P.O. Box 667
Layton, Utah 84041

Orders: 1.800.835.4993
www.gibbs-smith.com

Designed by Dawn DeVries Sokol
Printed and bound in China
Gibbs Smith books are printed on either recycled, 100% post-consumer waste, FSC-certified papers
or on paper produced from a 100% certified sustainable forest/controlled wood source.

Library of Congress Cataloging-in-Publication Data

Herrick, Holly.
   Southern farmers market cookbook / Holly Herrick ; photographs by Rick McKee. — 1st ed.
      p. cm.
   Includes index.
   ISBN-13: 978-1-4236-0474-7
   ISBN-10: 1-4236-0474-1
   1. Cookery (Natural foods) 2. Farmers' markets. 3. Cookery, American—Southern style. I. Title.
TX741.H468 2009
641.5'636—dc22
                           2008036452

To the tenders of the earth; to the quiet, behind-the-scenes, and mostly unheralded bearers of Mother Earth's bounty. To small farmers everywhere who work diligently for little money yet nurture, cultivate, and bring forth the priceless rewards of fresh and sustainable gems of the seasons. And especially to the small farmers of the South, who achieve all of this with the added burdens of a scorching summer sun, long, fickle seasons, while maintaining a storied agrarian tradition.

CONTENTS

PREFACE

The seeds for this book were probably sown thirty-five years ago when I was a little girl growing up in a rural area west of Boston. There, I, my twin sister, and two older brothers lived, grew, played, and worked on thirty-two acres of open land, rolling pastures, and forest. My mother rather poetically referred to the place, aka Peach Hill Farm, as a "gentleman's farm."

There were times, I assure you, that felt anything but gentlemanly on our little farm. For instance, cleaning out the chicken coop and collecting eggs on hot, putrid Saturday mornings (a weekly chore) or hauling what seemed like a ton of potatoes up a large hill from our vegetable garden to the house. I think my "city" friends felt a little sorry for us. As much as I loved my little rural paradise, sometimes I did, too.

But in hindsight, many years later, I realize we were the lucky ones. There, we learned to value things that so many children—those born during the plasticine, packaged food decades that followed WWII and raged through the consumer-driven 1970s, 80s, and much of the 90s—did not. We learned that hard work eventually guaranteed easy play, a healthy appetite for fresh, simple food, and long nights of silent, deep sleep. We learned that if we did not waste, we would not want. We knew the aroma of a carrot that came fresh out of the ground—ground we had tilled and seeded with our own hands. We knew the simple pleasure of eating a boiled egg that had been gathered from the chicken coop that morning. The lessons and acquired tastes of those early years have endured. As I grew older and lived and worked in many different cities, from Boston to Paris, I cultivated them by shopping at and supporting farmers markets.

In rural France, surrounded by daily farmers markets in neighboring villages, I learned to shop like the natives, buying only what I needed for a few days and returning to stock up on more freshness when my 3-foot-tall refrigerator was empty. When I moved to Charleston, South Carolina, in 2000, the tiny downtown Charleston Farmers Market was composed of a handful of vendors and situated in a narrow alley. Now, it's situated on the grounds of a large, central park called Marion Square and swells with nearly one hundred vendors and twenty-one farmers touting an ever-increasing variety of wares. This colorful market—like most I visited across the Southeast while writing this book—boasts grass-fed beef, local seafood, locally prepared bread, cheese, certified organic produce, and sustainably grown produce.

In this book, I attempt to explain why it is important, rewarding, nutritious, eco-friendly, communally supportive, fun, and, at times, spiritual, to shop at local farmers markets. It provides descriptions of the produce, farmers, and markets of eight core Southern states: South Carolina, North Carolina, Georgia, Alabama, Mississippi, Florida, Kentucky, and Tennessee.

On a 3,000-mile plus odyssey, I observed trends and met farmers at twenty-some select markets, big and small, independent and state-run.

Everywhere, we savored fresh food and the changing vistas of the region, from the rise of the mountains of North Carolina and Kentucky and the bow of the rolling, leafy plains of Northern Alabama to the flatlands of the Mississippi Delta, Northern Florida, and South Carolina, and the Georgia Lowcountry.

Though the players may change, the name of the farmers-market game remains the same: *buy local, buy right.* No matter where you live, it is my sincere hope that this book will help you to shop locally and seasonally. The timing and fruits of the seasons in Albany are far different from those in Atlanta, but the reasons for finding and buying them are exactly the same. So, in many ways, this book is intended to be a guide for better local and farmers market shopping that extends beyond any particular region and expands into a better national and international "buying local" perspective.

I wish happy shopping to all fellow farmers-market fans and to those who may someday become one of them.

INTRODUCTION
SOUTHERN FARMERS MARKETS— FEEDING THE FRENZY

MERCIFULLY, THE OLD ADAGE IS TRUE.
The more things change, the more they stay the same.

It seems the whole world is at last reawakening to the simple, nutritional, and unselfish joys of drinking from the bountiful cup of sustainable, local farming. These people are, I think, a bit like me—that eight-year-old girl in central Massachusetts, so many years ago, who revered the farm-raised carrot but never really excelled at growing her own.

Whole generations brought up on plastic-wrapped white bread and frozen dinners in a rushing, wasteful, impatient, consumer-driven culture are yearning to get back to the basics. They're aching to get closer to the silent, timeless wisdom of the earth and to their very souls. They want to know their food—where it came from, who grew it, and how it was grown. Then, they want to go home and cook it, savor it, and sit back, feeling nurtured and happy they've done something good for themselves, the earth, and small farmers.

"I think [this desire] is because we've gotten away from [the source]. The whole chicken nuggets shaped like a dinosaur thing in the grocery store—it's a turnoff. People have no connection with where their food is coming from and they want to be closer to it," says Suzanne Welander, communications director of Georgia Organics, a nonprofit organization for the state of Georgia that leads the state's "Buy Local for the State" campaign.

"There is a real yearning for local, that's for sure. Sixty percent of organic farming in this country is in California. That's over 2,000 miles away, so by the time it gets here, it's not very appealing. Surveys have shown that people want fresh and they want flavor. The second reason people want to buy local is to support local farmers," says Welander. "[Farmers markets] are a place where food has a face and a place, and [they] allow you to connect with other people there. It's enriching and nourishing and helps you maintain your relationship to the land. That's lost in a grocery," she adds.

This connection can be found and sustained by shopping regularly at local farmers markets. Maybe that's why they're growing so quickly in popularity. According to the USDA, in 2007 there were more than 4,500 farmers markets in the United States, nearly double the number of nationwide farmers markets that existed in 2000. Sales from these markets exceeded $1 billion, most of which went back to the pockets of small farmers.

In the South, where deeply entrenched economic-agrarian roots date back to the Colonial era and growing seasons are longer than most other parts of the country, small farming is big business. A study (Farms,

Land in Farms and Livestock Operations, 2007 Summary) conducted by the National Agricultural Statistics Service (NASS) showed that the South (in this study defined as Texas, Arkansas, Louisiana, Michigan, Mississippi, Alabama, Tennessee, Georgia, Florida, South Carolina, North Carolina, Kentucky, Virginia, Maryland, and the greater Washington, D.C. area) makes up 42.1 percent of the farms in the entire United States—the largest regional farming segment in the country. But geography dictates that farm sizes in the South (and Northeast) are smaller. "This translates to smaller farms and more intimate farm production in these regions," explains NASS statistician Scott Shimmin.

In a 2005 report, the NASS revealed that the South's largest economic sales class was farmers earning between $1,000 and $99,999—in other words, small farmers. These are the same guys and gals who rely on selling their goods at farmers markets in order to survive. Yet the NASS found in its 2007 summary that the number of farms in this income range actually declined that year—"a result of operations moving to larger sales classes by consolidation or expansion and strong commodity prices." This is another way of saying that large, mass-production farming is more profitable to a farmer's bottom line. But that's not to say it's necessarily conducive to getting the freshest,

least chemically manipulated food in your shopping basket or your body.

Despite a variety of government, business, and grass root initiatives being implemented across the South to increase consumer awareness about the importance of buying local and urging consumers to support venues (including grocery stores and restaurants) that do so, farmers markets remain the economic bread and butter for Southern small farmers. "The farmers market is absolutely essential for 90 percent, if not 95 percent of our farmers, says Sarah Blacklin, market manager of Carrboro Farmers Market in Carrboro, North Carolina. "They really put their life into making sure this market has integrity. It basically has been the best-selling market for all of our vendors. This is where they make their weekly sales."

As if small farmers' dependence on these markets to make a living and supporting local farmers is not reason enough to shop at local farmers markets, let's explore some of the other reasons, both tangible and intangible.

SEVEN TANGIBLE REASONS TO SHOP AT LOCAL FARMERS MARKETS:

1. By establishing a relationship with farmers market vendors, which is a natural progression as a regular shopper, you know where your food is coming from and how it was raised. This is comforting in an

age when mass *E. coli* and/or salmonella outbreaks in commercially raised produce and tainted seafood from overseas is commonplace.

2. Shopping local, defined by most Southern farmers markets as anything grown up to 100 miles away (in some markets, it's 50 miles or less), reduces the need for cross-country shipping or storage, which helps save precious fuel and is kinder to the environment.

3. Buying local helps preserve biodiversity with the increased use of heirloom varieties that, as one farmer told me, "were designed to grow where they're planted, not to grow elsewhere." This means there are more varieties of produce to choose from and also that growing them is less taxing on the environment. Because they're not designed for early picking, long shipments or long shelf-life, they're good to the earth and good for you. Also, because local farmers must react to seasonal weather, their fields are turned over more frequently, which promotes a more nutrient-rich soil that ultimately yields more nutritious food.

4. You can enjoy fresher, more nutritious, and significantly less chemically treated food that's usually harvested (when local) within twenty-four hours of purchase. In some cases, the food is certified organic. Local food is grown with minimal wax, growth hormones, pesticides, nitrogen, and storage-related chemicals. It tastes like food, not chemicals—a true breath of fresh air.

5. Buying local keeps money local and helps support individual communities, thereby increasing the quality of community life.

6. Buying local also helps maintain the rural integrity of neighboring lands and farms. Supporting local is supporting local farmland. Because many small growers practice certified organic or largely organic farming practices, synthetic compounds and preservatives are not present in their fields or in their foods. Even for the small farmers that do use some chemicals, ultimately they use significantly less than those used and practically mandated by larger commercial growers.

7. Buying direct from the farmer at farmers markets means fair and direct transactions, without the wallet-minimizing middleman. Also, buying seasonally means you're not paying extra money for products that have been shipped halfway across the world, so you're getting better, fresh-picked produce for less.

SEVEN INTANGIBLE REASONS TO SHOP AT LOCAL FARMERS MARKETS

Some of the reasons listed in "tangibles" could also apply to the benefits of buying locally at a grocer or other outlet, but each of the following is exclusive to farmers markets.

1. To breathe fresh air and (hopefully) feel the sunshine on your back.

2. To interact with other members of the town and the community. To talk and listen, to learn, and possibly to make new friends.

3. To stop and smell the roses, or the fire-roasted pizza (prepared with local produce), or a pint of fresh strawberries, or whatever delights you encounter at the market. This is living, not playing a game on the computer or talking on a cell phone.

4. To teach yourself, your children, your spouse or your friend about the difference in taste and quality between a crisp, heirloom apple and a stale, waxed, imported variety. To see what real food is and to meet the real people who grew it and probably were up well before dawn to harvest and bring it to market.

5. To appreciate the value of raw, unprocessed or minimally processed foods and develop a healthy taste for them. This is an especially important lesson for children.

6. To absorb the gorgeous visuals, like the morning sun shining through the local honey and dappling a bouquet of wild flowers.

7. To laugh and have fun. Life is short!

LET'S GO SHOPPING
TOSS THE LIST AND TAP INTO YOUR SENSES

One absolutely cannot and must not go to a farmers market with a shopping list in hand or with a rigid menu fixed in one's head. This mindset defies everything these markets are about—seasonal, fresh inspiration—and wholly robs the experience of the pure cooking liberation and fun these markets afford at every turn.

Instead, put an open, curious mind as the single item on your list and jump in with seasonally inspired, sensual abandon. Breathe in the freshness, see and touch (but always ask first!) the colors and textures, talk with the farmers, know your likes and dislikes; let all of these things help design your meal.

Allow yourself to think differently than you may have in the past. Instead of you dictating what you're going to buy and prepare, the market's seasonal, picked-just-that-morning bounty dictates it for you.

For example, you're loosely thinking about making a spinach omelet for supper and you get to market and discover the spinach is less than fresh, out of season, or not in stock, and then come upon some incredible arugula or tat soi. Embrace this opportunity to rework your plan! It's more fun than Christmas morning, and the presents come in new and different edible packages every day of the season.

Of course, shopping, thinking, and cooking like this takes some practice and a well-stocked home pantry (see suggestions in the Farmers Market Home Pantry, page 15). Some knowledge of basic cooking techniques doesn't hurt, either. This is because the earth tenders you'll come across at farmers markets need to be handled with care and a less-is-more approach. After all, it takes very little cooking and gloss to coax the glorious flavor out of a beautiful beet. If you know a little about roasting and basic vinaigrette preparation, you'll be in good stead to take on this minimalist challenge and make a fabulous meal.

In this book, I provide ample input on technique in the recipes, but novice cooks may want to begin with a more complete culinary-technique reference book. Find a good source and study it a little bit every day and you will become a better, more confident, and happier cook.

There are a few things, besides your open mind, that you should consider bringing with you to the farmers market and a few things you should consider not bringing. Here goes:

WHAT TO BRING TO MARKET:

- Cash is king at most farmers markets. While some vendors do take credit cards, all are more comfortable with cash. It makes for an easier, faster transaction and frees their hands and minds for the next sale or conversation. Usually, I'm shopping for myself or a small group. I always bring more than I think I will need, just in case. I suggest you do the same.

- You'll need something practical, maneuverable, and preferably biodegradable or eco-friendly to carry your farmers market bounty. I have a friend whom I regularly see at the market with a roll-cart that resembles a carry-on style suitcase. I opt for a broad, shallow, and sturdy basket with a handle. Its flat bottom is well-suited for arranging tender greens, berries, eggs, flowers, and more in their own safe space in the basket, and it is deep enough to layer if necessary. Avoid very deep or floppy bags, if you can. It's easy to crush the goods if they're stacked too deeply.

WHAT NOT TO BRING TO MARKET:

- A wallet or purse is not necessary and can be cumbersome in more ways than one. Leave them secured in the trunk of your car or at home if you've walked or biked.

- Think twice or thrice about unruly, ill-behaved children or pets. While both are ostensibly welcome at most farmers markets (with the exception of the latter at some enclosed market spaces), they're not necessarily enjoyed by all. Farmers markets provide an outstanding cultural, nutritional, and social educational experience for children, and I encourage you to bring yours along whenever you can. Just be sure they respect the space of those around them. The same goes for your dog, or your parrot (yes, I've seen one of these out and about), or your pet of whatever feather. Farmers markets provide a great opportunity for your dog (especially) to socialize and spend a lovely, aroma-rich morning or afternoon. I regularly bring my cocker spaniel, Tann Mann, to the market. But, because he can have space issues, I only bring him during off hours, when it's less crowded, and on days when I have the time to really keep my eye on him. In general, it helps to know your dog and treat him accordingly. Always be respectful of other people and dogs—and don't forget to bring a baggie to pick up any pooch (or parrot!) surprises.

A FARMERS MARKET HOME PANTRY

MORE AND MORE, FARMERS MARKETS provide a nearly one-stop shopping experience. Happily, far removed from generic "super stores," many non-produce specific staples—local eggs, honey, fresh herbs, cheeses, beef, pork, chicken, seafood, pasta, grits, rice, bread, canned goods, jellies, and more—are readily available at many farmers markets across the South and the country.

Still, in order to be the most liberated, inspired, and versatile farmers market cook you can be, a well-stocked home larder is a necessity. Having staples within easy reach when you get home with your market cache will allow you to create complete, nutritional meals without having to make a mad dash at the last second for the crucial ingredient to complete what would be an otherwise unfettered meal.

Strangely, I find I make the best meals and create the best recipes when I have the least products on hand or the least time to think either over in advance. Life is a little bit like that, too, I suppose. Less analysis opens the door to more peace and creativity. I find it very helpful to have most of the following items around at all times. Pick and choose whatever works for you. It's an initial investment to stock a pantry, but like good quality cookware and knives, it will pay culinary dividends for years to come. Many of these items are commonly available at seasonal Southern farmers markets.

DAIRY: Whole cream, half-and-half, milk, sour cream/creme fraiche, sweet butter, aged cheeses—Parmigiano-Reggiano, asiago, assorted fresh or semi-aged cheeses

EGGS: A fresh dozen on hand at all times

SPICES/HERBS

Spices: Allspice, cayenne, cinnamon, cloves, cumin, curry, fennel, ginger, nutmeg, paprika, pepper (black and white), red pepper flakes, salt (kosher or sea), vanilla pods/quality pure vanilla extract

Herbs: Basil, bay leaves, chervil, herbes de Provence, marjoram, mint, oregano, parsley (curly or Italian), rosemary, sage, tarragon, thyme

BAKING/GENERAL COOKING: Flour (all-purpose, bread, whole wheat), baking soda, baking powder, chocolate (semisweet, dark, and milk), sugar (granulated, brown, powdered), molasses, honey, yeast, raisins, currants, assorted dried fruits, coffee

NUTS: Almonds, walnuts, macadamia nuts, pecans, pignoli nuts, peanuts

OILS: Vegetable, canola, olive, extra virgin olive, walnut

VINEGARS: Balsamic, red/white wine, apple cider, champagne, rice

WINE/JUICES: Good-quality red and white wines, fresh orange juice, lemons, limes, raw apple cider, pomegranate juice

LIQUOR: Vermouth (dry/sweet), Marsala

LEGUMES: Assorted canned/dried lentils, split peas, garbanzo beans, kidney beans, black beans, black-eyed/yellow-eyed peas, navy beans

GRAINS/SEEDS: Brown rice, basmati rice, Arborio rice, Carolina Gold rice, quinoa, flax seed, grits, barley, bulgur

DRIED PASTA: Couscous, assorted whole grain and regular pasta shapes and sizes

STOCK: Good-quality canned/boxed or homemade chicken, vegetable, and beef stocks

CANNED GOODS: White albacore tuna packed in water, peanut butter, cashew butter

MEATS: Bacon, sausage

CONDIMENTS: Dijon mustard, whole grain mustard, hot mustard, ketchup, Worcestershire sauce, Tabasco Sauce, A-1 Sauce, horseradish, mayonnaise, pickle relish

FOUR THINGS I CAN'T EVER BE WITHOUT: Onions, celery, carrots, and garlic. These "aromats" are the backbone of good cooking and are used frequently throughout this book.

HOW TO USE THIS BOOK

ULTIMATELY, THIS BOOK IS DESIGNED to help you evolve into a more informed and inspired farmers market shopper and seasonal cook of locally grown or produced foods.

With one (noted) exception, the original recipes were created based upon my many visits over the past decade to Southern farmers markets. Many have previously been printed in *The Post and Courier*, Charleston's daily newspaper, for my Market Whimsy column, or in other (noted) magazines. Many were created "fresh" for this book.

All of them are included to provide information, ideas, and general frameworks for using season-specific produce and farmers market products. They are not necessarily intended to be followed stringently, but viewed with the same open mind you bring with you to shop and visit farmers markets. This is what makes cooking fun! All recipes in this book have been measured and tested to a tee, with one seasoning exception. As a rule, I do not measure salt and pepper at all in order to invite you to season according to your taste and to

encourage you to season ingredients in layers. If you do so, and taste all along the way, your food will taste better.

The recipes are gathered in traditional appetizer, soup, salads/sides, main courses, and dessert categories. To assist readers in following the seasons, each recipe is grouped into its relevant season and organized and marked accordingly. Since this book covers a vast regional territory with seasonal and temperature variations of its own, these seasonal labels are generalized, with a grain of salt for the region. More specific state-defined seasonality charts as well as resources for finding farmers market listings within each state are provided as references at the back of the book.

Along the way you will find storage/usage tips and historical/cultural information about various ingredients, many of them specific to the South. It is my hope the markets and the farmers that stock them will come to life in your heart and mind, ultimately inspiring you to bring their fruits to culinary splendor in your very own kitchen.

SUPER STARTERS

SPRING, EARLY SUMMER, AND FALL

Fredrik's Celebrated Zucchini Toasts 20

Greek-Kissed Stuffed Zucchini Blossoms 22

SUMMER

Cantaloupe Balls with Prosciutto, Lime, and Basil 23

WBAM! Watermelon, Bacon, Avocado, and Fresh Goat Cheese Sandwich Bites 24

SUMMER THROUGH FALL

Butter Bean and Grape Tomato Bruschetta 25

Roasted Guinea Eggplant and Garlic Dip 26

FALL THROUGH WINTER

Chow-Chow Deviled White Shrimp and Farm Fresh Eggs 28

Hot and Happy Holiday Cider 32

FREDRIK'S CELEBRATED ZUCCHINI TOASTS

My long-standing tennis instructor, Fredrik, is not Southern. He is Swedish. However, he and his French/German wife, Nadja, share a deep love of good food, especially fresh vegetables, seafood, and chocolate. Over the years, we've become friends and as such have shared recipe ideas—one of our most loved subjects.

This is my interpretation of one of Fredrik and Nadja's favorites. They like it so much that they prepared it for their wedding guests. It's such a brilliant, fresh twist on this prolific and delicious summer squash, I think it will become one of your favorites, as well. Grating, salting, and draining the zucchini helps extract water and concentrates the clean-tasting sweetness of the squash.

FOR THE TOPPING

2 large zucchini squash

1 teaspoon kosher or sea salt

2 tablespoons extra virgin olive oil

8 leaves fresh basil, chopped

3 cloves garlic

1 shallot, finely chopped

Salt and freshly ground pepper

FOR THE TOASTS

2 tablespoons butter

2 tablespoons olive oil

1 baguette French bread (or another favorite bread of choice), sliced and cut on the bias into 1/4-inch-thick pieces

Salt and freshly ground pepper

1/2 cup grated or shaved Parmigiano-Reggiano (or another aged hard cheese)

Fresh basil leaves or chopped tomatoes, to garnish

To prepare the topping, scrub and trim the tops and bases from the zucchini. Using a medium-size grater, grate over a bowl. Toss with the salt and let stand 10 minutes. Rinse away the salt thoroughly and drain well in a colander. Shape the grated zucchini into tennis ball–size handfuls and squeeze out excess water; discard the water and return zucchini to the bowl. Toss with olive oil, basil, garlic, and shallot. Season with salt and pepper to taste. Cover and allow to sit for at least 30 minutes before serving. (**NOTE:** The topping can be prepared up to this point and refrigerated, covered, for up to 24 hours.)

To prepare the toasts, heat a large skillet over medium-high heat. Add butter and oil and cook until just bubbling. Arrange bread slices in a single layer in the pan (you will need to do this in batches) and season generously with salt and pepper. Cook until golden on one side. Turn, season, and repeat. Remove the toasts from the pan and cool on a paper towel. (**NOTE:** The toasts will store, once cooled, in an airtight container for up to 2 days.)

To assemble, preheat the broiler and bring the zucchini mixture to room temperature. Scoop a scant tablespoon onto each prepared toast. Arrange the toasts in a single layer on a baking sheet. Broil on the middle rack of the oven until bubbling. Arrange on a platter and sprinkle each toast with the cheese and garnish with basil or tomato. Serve immediately.

Makes 16–20 servings

ZUCCHINI PICKING

Look for blemish-free squash that is heavy for its size. Stay away from huge zucchini, as they can be stringy, bland, and tough. Use zucchini as soon as you bring it home for an extra-special fresh treat. If you need to store zucchini, store it loosely wrapped in plastic or cloth in the refrigerator for one to three days. The same rules apply for yellow summer squash.

GREEK-KISSED STUFFED ZUCCHINI BLOSSOMS

It took me years of combing farmers markets and ample coaxing from multiple market vendors to summon the courage to work with the impossibly delicate, seductive flowers of zucchini squash. Like newborn babies, they frightened me with their seeming fragility and seamless beauty.

One try and I was converted. In fact, both the male and female blossoms of the zucchini plant are surprisingly simple to work with, assuming you use them the day you buy them. After that, they start wilting and become tough, which makes them harder to work with and robs them of their peak culinary power.

Chopped olives, oregano, and lemon give this recipe a touch of the sunny flavors of Greece, but feel free to play with this and have fun as you gain blossom bravado.

12 zucchini blossoms

¼ cup cream cheese, at room temperature (or substitute fresh goat cheese)

¼ cup whole milk ricotta cheese

1 tablespoon half-and-half

Salt and freshly ground pepper

1 tablespoon chopped fresh parsley

1 teaspoon chopped fresh oregano

Zest of 1 lemon

2 tablespoons finely chopped pitted Greek olives

1 egg yolk

1½ cups all-purpose flour

2 cups vegetable oil

Gently rinse the blossoms in cool water and trim the stem length to 2 inches. Pat dry, very gently, with a paper towel; set aside. Using a hand mixer, whip together the cream cheese, ricotta, half-and-half, and salt and pepper to taste in a medium-size bowl until light and frothy. With a spatula, fold in the parsley, oregano, lemon zest, and olives. Taste and adjust seasonings if necessary. Gently stuff each blossom with about 2 tablespoons of the stuffing mixture, depending on the blossom's size. Do not overfill! Gently twist the petals together at the top of the blossom to seal; set aside.

In a small shallow bowl, beat the egg yolk. In a second, larger shallow bowl, combine the flour with some salt and pepper to season. To coat each blossom, individually dip in the egg yolk, and then coat lightly in the flour to cover all surfaces.

To fry the stuffed blossoms, heat the oil to 375 degrees, lightly sizzling in a large, deep skillet over medium-high heat. Cook the stuffed blossoms in batches (about 4 at a time), gently spooning them into the oil and cooking on each side for about 3 minutes, or until light golden brown. Remove, drain on paper towels, and season very lightly with salt. Serve immediately on a platter garnished with a fresh zucchini blossom and/or fresh oregano. (Prediction: They'll be gone in about 2 minutes, so be prepared for the next course!)

CANTALOUPE BALLS
WITH PROSCIUTTO, LIME, AND BASIL

On a hot Southern summer morning, the luscious smell of ripe cantaloupe at a farmers market booth will reach your nose even before your eyes fall upon the gentle fruit. Simple and unadulterated, the classic pairing of sweet, fragrant melon and salty aged ham sparkles with a fresh twist of lime and a drizzle of chopped fresh basil. Serve this as an appetizer to a light, midsummer evening meal. Be open to variations using watermelon and honeydew, which work equally well with the lime, basil, and ham in this recipe.

½ large cantaloupe, seeded

½ pound prosciutto or aged ham, thinly sliced

Juice of ½ lime, plus juices from the cantaloupe

3 tablespoons good-quality extra virgin olive oil

Freshly ground pepper

3 tablespoons chopped fresh basil

Using a mellon-baller or rounded spoon, scoop balls from the seeded half of the melon and then place in a bowl, reserving any of the melon's juices. Cut the prosciutto into ¼-inch-wide strips and wrap once around each melon ball. Seal the ends by piercing through them and the melon ball with a toothpick. Chill, covered, up to 3 hours. Just before serving, drizzle the reserved melon juices, lime juice, oil, and pepper over top. Toss to coat. Arrange on an attractive serving platter and sprinkle with the basil. Serve cool to room temperature.

Makes about 40 bite-size servings

WBAM! WATERMELON, BACON,
AVOCADO, AND FRESH GOAT CHEESE SANDWICH BITES

Summer absolutely sizzles in the South. Watermelon is a refreshing and popular way to chill out, and it takes on major taste and texture proportions in this fun twist on a white-bread BLT. At once crunchy, salty, sweet, cool, and creamy, this sandwich can be eaten in either appetizer portions or as an easy summer lunch.

Technically, avocados aren't local since they're not grown in the region, but watermelon, fresh bread, goat cheese, and, in some cases, bacon are readily available at many farmers markets. Prepare these just before serving to avoid soggy sandwiches. They will not sit around long—I promise.

1 fresh French baguette, cut into four 4-inch lengths, and then halved horizontally

$\frac{1}{4}$ cup olive oil

12 slices bacon

1 ripe avocado

Juice of $\frac{1}{2}$ lime

8 ounces fresh goat cheese

Salt and freshly ground pepper

1 small, seedless watermelon, cut into 8 ($\frac{1}{4}$-inch-thick) slices and chilled

16 fresh basil leaves

4 teaspoons Dijon mustard

4 teaspoons mayonnaise

Preheat broiler to high. Lay the baguettes, cut-side up, on a single layer of a baking sheet. Drizzle evenly with the oil. Watching closely, broil on the middle rack of the oven until golden brown, about 5 minutes. Remove and set aside to cool. Meanwhile, cook the bacon in a very large sauté pan. Remove bacon from the pan and drain on paper towels.

To assemble, cut the avocado in half, remove the pit, and cut each half into 4 thick slices. Drizzle evenly with the lime juice. Spread one-quarter of the goat cheese on the bottom half of each section of toasted bread. Season each with a bit of salt and pepper. Arrange 3 pieces of bacon on top, followed by 2 slices watermelon, then 2 slices avocado. Arrange 4 basil leaves on top. Slather mustard and mayonnaise in equal quantities on one side of each remaining slice of bread. Place on top of the sandwiches. To make "bites," cut each sandwich into 4 pieces and secure by piercing each section with a sturdy toothpick and serve immediately.

*Makes 16 sandwich bites
(or 4 regular sandwiches)*

BUTTER BEAN AND GRAPE TOMATO BRUSCHETTA

Butter beans have a mild flavor and a meaty texture, so they play with a virtually endless combination of flavors, from goat cheese to bacon. Here, I mix them with sprite grape tomatoes and serve on toast for a play on a classic bruschetta. For a fabulous salad, leave out the bruschetta toast. The flavors deepen with time, so prepare the bean mixture several hours ahead and assemble just before serving. Serve at room temperature for maximum flavor.

FOR THE SALAD

2 cups water

3 tablespoons salt

1 cup fresh butter beans

¼ cup good-quality extra virgin olive oil

2 cloves garlic, minced

¼ medium red onion, finely chopped

½ cup quartered (lengthwise) grape tomatoes, or finely chopped regular tomato

2 tablespoons red wine vinegar

2 tablespoons chopped fresh parsley

2 tablespoons chopped fresh basil

1 teaspoon finely grated lemon, orange, or lime zest

Salt and freshly ground pepper

FOR THE TOAST

1 country-style baguette

3 tablespoons good-quality extra virgin olive oil

Salt and freshly ground pepper

3 cloves garlic, peeled and lightly smashed

Bring the water and salt to a boil in a medium pot. Add the beans, reduce heat to a simmer, and cook until crisp-tender, about 25 minutes depending on freshness. Drain in a colander, rinsing thoroughly with cold water. In a large bowl, combine the cooked beans with remaining salad ingredients. Season carefully and taste to verify seasoning. Cover and allow to marinate at room temperature up to 4 hours or refrigerate overnight and bring back to room temperature before serving.

To prepare the toast, preheat the oven to 450 degrees. Cut the baguette into ¼-inch-thick slices at a diagonal angle. Arrange in a single layer on a baking sheet. Drizzle with half of the oil, season generously with salt and pepper, turn over and repeat on the other side. Place in the center rack of the oven. Bake until golden brown, about 5 to 8 minutes, turn over and repeat, being careful not to burn the toast. Remove from the oven. While still warm, rub both sides of each toast with the smashed garlic.

To serve, spoon about 2 tablespoons of the butter bean salad on each warm toast. Arrange on a large platter and garnish with fresh parsley or basil points. Serve immediately.

NOTE: The bruschetta toast can be prepared up to one day in advance, cooled and stored in an airtight container. To "crisp" the toasts, reheat in a 450-degree oven for just a few minutes and serve as outlined above.

Makes about 16–20 servings

ROASTED GUINEA EGGPLANT AND GARLIC DIP

The Guinea squash—the deep purple-to-black, large, traditional eggplant—is significantly more bitter than the sweet and tender varieties such as Japanese, zebra, and neon eggplants that grace Southern farmers markets from summer through the first frost of fall. That is why it is a perfect candidate for roasting, which sweetens the flesh and makes for easy bitter-skin removal after it's out of the oven.

This is a delicious, nutritious low-calorie dish that makes use of eggplant's natural tendency to soak up just about anything as readily as a six-year-old soaks up knowledge and bad words. In this case, the eggplant is exposed to heaping doses of sweet roasted garlic, yogurt, fruity olive oil, and lemon.

2 medium-size Guinea
    eggplants
1 head garlic
Juice of 1 lemon
3 tablespoons chopped fresh
    parsley
¼ cup plain yogurt
¼ cup extra virgin olive oil
Dash hot pepper flakes
Salt and freshly ground pepper

Preheat oven to 425 degrees. Slice the eggplants in half vertically and arrange them, cut-side down, on a roasting pan. Trim the papery top of the garlic, drizzle with a dash of olive oil and wrap tightly with foil. Place on the roasting pan beside the eggplant. Roast until the eggplant has softened and collapsed upon itself and the garlic is tender to the touch; about 25 minutes. Set both aside until they're cool enough to handle, about 15 minutes.

Cup one eggplant half in your free hand and scoop the soft, juicy flesh away from the skin, reserving any juices. Repeat with other half and place the flesh and juices into the bowl of a food processor fitted with a steel blade. Squeeze the garlic cloves free from the skins of the entire head and add directly to the food processor bowl, discarding any papery skins. Add lemon juice, parsley, and yogurt and pulse until smooth, about 10 times. While the machine is running, gradually incorporate the olive oil in a steady, thin stream. Add the hot pepper flakes, salt, and pepper; pulse to incorporate.

Refrigerate mixture overnight. Allow the dip to come to room temperature before serving and arrange in a pretty bowl surrounded by toasted pita bread wedges.

Makes 8–12 servings

CHOW-CHOW DEVILED WHITE SHRIMP AND FARM FRESH EGGS

This is the consummate fall farmers market dish and it's oh-so Southern and oh-so good. From September through December, the waters off Charleston, Savannah, and Beaufort are teeming with milky, sweet white shrimp. Many argue that the white shrimp's flavor is nuttier than its summer brown shrimp counterpart and the texture is decidedly meatier. Of course, you could substitute brown shrimp, but the extra sweetness of white shrimp works especially well with the rich yolk flavor of fresh eggs and the tangy bite of chow-chow. When lovingly combined, these ingredients will render this recipe a favorite in your crowd-pleaser cooking arsenal. It is definitely a favorite of mine.

TO COOK THE EGGS

6 fresh eggs, at room
   temperature
Water to cover

TO COOK THE SHRIMP

10 to 12 white shrimp, shells on
3 sprigs fresh thyme
1 bay leaf
1 tablespoon salt
1/4 cup good-quality dry white
   wine
Water to cover

FOR THE FILLING

Reserved yolks from the
   cooked eggs
2 tablespoons chow-chow
   (look for a locally canned
   variety at your farmers
   market)
Dash of red wine vinegar
1 tablespoon mayonnaise
1/2 teaspoon Dijon mustard
Salt and freshly ground pepper
10 chives, cut into 1/2-inch
   lengths, to garnish

Place the eggs in a single layer in a medium-size pot. Cover with tepid tap water. Bring the water to a boil over high heat. Once boiling, remove the pan from the heat, cover, and allow the eggs to sit in the hot water for exactly 17 minutes.

Meanwhile, in a deep skillet, prepare the shrimp. Combine the shrimp, thyme, bay leaf, salt, wine, and enough water to cover. Bring to a boil over high heat, reduce to a simmer, and cook until the shrimp are just opaque in the center, about 3 minutes; drain. When cool enough to handle, peel and discard the shells. Coarsely chop eight of the shrimp; cut the other shrimp into 1/2-inch lengths to garnish the top of the eggs; set both aside.

After the eggs have stood in the water for a full 17 minutes, remove them from the water (but don't pour the water out), and transfer the eggs to a bowl of ice water. Chill for 2 minutes. Put the eggs back in cooking water and bring the cooking water up to a boil for 10 seconds; then return the eggs to the ice water. Chill for 15 minutes before peeling.

Once they have chilled, peel the eggs and cut each in half lengthwise. Carefully scoop out the yolks, smashing and blending them thoroughly with a fork in a small bowl. Set aside the egg white halves.

continued on page 30

Whisk all the remaining filling ingredients except the shrimp and chives into the egg yolks. Taste carefully to verify seasoning. Fold in the chopped shrimp. Scoop a generous tablespoon of filling into each egg-white half, topping each with reserved shrimp pieces and 3 to 4 chive cuttings for garnish. Chill and serve within several hours.

(This recipe was originally published in the September/October 2006 edition of Lowcountry Living Magazine*)*.

Serves 12

EGG TIMER

The reason for the apparently complicated cooking time and chilling/heating/chilling process for the eggs, which I borrowed from Julia Child, is two-fold and well worth the effort. First, it prevents the ugly gray hue that can form around the cooked yolk if it is overcooked. More importantly, the expansion and contraction process makes peeling fresh eggs, and all eggs for that matter, much less troublesome.

THE SCOOP ON CHOW-CHOW

Depending on who you ask or to which food history source you reference, chow-chow originally came to this country via trades with China (some sources also include India). The name is of Chinese descent and refers to the combination of different mixtures of foods. In time, this became a motley and varied combination of vegetables, from cabbage to cukes to zucchini, which were packed together as a kind of sweet pickled relish. Similarly, in the South, a wide variety of vegetables are used, though cabbage is often a prominent player. Served on hot dogs and burgers or folded into chicken or tuna salad, it gives original zing, sweetness, and sometimes heat (not unlike the Korean version called kimchee) to anything with which it's mixed. A Southern staple, variations on chow-chow can be found at most farmers markets throughout the Southeast. Sample them widely to find your personal favorite. It's great to have some at-the-ready in your larder.

GO WILD FOR AMERICAN SHRIMP!

Close to 85 percent of the shrimp consumed in this country is imported, the bulk of it pond-raised. Initiatives such as Certified Wild American Shrimp are helping to get local, wild shrimp from the waters of North Carolina, South Carolina, Georgia, Florida, Alabama, Mississippi, Louisiana, and Texas to our tables, restaurants and farmers markets, all the while promoting sustainability, preserving freshness, and protecting a sacred Southern culinary and cultural tradition.

Equally important, the taste of wild, local Southern shrimp is incomparable and unmistakable. Sweet, nutty, salty, with all kinds of variations depending on the type of shrimp and the season (which varies by state), it's light years removed from the bland, watery-palate wasteland of most imported shrimp.

Shrimp (and other local seafood) seasons vary by state. Here's what's local and where, according to Wild American Shrimp, Inc.:

White Shrimp: Flourish in brackish waters and estuaries and feed on crustaceans and seaweed, yielding a sweet, distinct flavor.

Brown Shrimp: Found along salt marshes and mud bottoms of the Atlantic and Gulf coasts and feed on kelp. Their flavor is salty, like the sea, and potent.

Pink Shrimp: The most delicate of the local Southern shrimp trifecta, these rosy crustaceans are prolific near Florida and the Gulf coast.

HOT AND HAPPY HOLIDAY CIDER

You either love eggnog or you hate it. I hate it, with or without rum. For me, it's too cloying, too sweet, too rich—not to mention fattening. However, put on a pot of fresh cider—free of added sugar, preservatives, and water—to simmer with cinnamon and some citrus and you've got instant Christmas and a refreshing alternative for an alcohol-free holiday (or anytime) libation.

Fresh ciders can be found in myriad flavors (I've encountered apple, peach, Black Bing cherry) throughout the farmers market season. Start simmering the cider about an hour before your guests arrive, as it will fill the house with an inviting, happy aroma that sets the stage for a good time to be had by all. If you prefer to lighten things up with a bit of booze, a splash of vodka is delicious, too.

2 liters fresh cider (Black Bing cherry, apple, peach—your choice)

1 orange, thinly sliced and seeds removed

1 lemon, thinly sliced and seeds removed

1 cinnamon stick

3 or 4 cloves

Combine all the ingredients in a large pot. Bring to a boil over high heat. Reduce to low and simmer until the citrus slices have softened and the mixture is fragrant, about 45 minutes. Serve hot in an attractive punch bowl and ladle into mugs. Best consumed in front of a blazing fire on a chilly night!

Serves 8–12

SULTRY SOUPS AND STEWS

WINTER THROUGH
EARLY SPRING
Comforting Cabbage Soup 36
Fresh Sweet Onion and Corn Chowder 38

LATE SPRING, SUMMER,
AND EARLY FALL
Cool Dill and Curry-Spiked
   Cucumber Soup 39

SUMMER
Sweet Corn and Crowder Pea Chowder 40

SUMMER THROUGH FALL
Curried Tomato and Okra Stew 42
Fresh Butter Bean and
   Smoked Ham Hock Soup 44

FALL
Meaty and Meatless Wild
   Mushroom Soup 46

FALL THROUGH WINTER
Buttercup Squash Soup with
   Fried Basil Leaves 48
Rich Roasted Pumpkin Soup
   with Fancy Spiced Croutons 50

FALL THROUGH SPRING
Hearty Sausage and Northern
   Bean Soup with Kale 51
Creamy White Turnip Soup with Spring
   Onions and Roasted Garlic 52

COMFORTING CABBAGE SOUP

Despite being light on calories and loaded with all kinds of good things including vitamin C, fiber, and antioxidants, cabbage gets a bad, stinky rap. This luxurious-tasting soup will change your mind about cabbage—forever! Sliced green cabbage goes delectably with a long, slow simmer in (preferably homemade) chicken stock and with the delicate touches of thyme, sweet vermouth, and salty ham hock.

Green cabbage stores well for several days to a week, wrapped loosely in plastic and stored in the vegetable compartment of the refrigerator. Be sure to remove any tough central stalks and cut the cabbage into long thin strips (or "julienne"; see Julienne Know-How, facing).

4 cups chicken stock

8 cups water

2 ham hocks

1 bay leaf

1 onion, peeled and finely sliced

1 medium head cabbage, trimmed and julienned

2 tablespoons butter

2 tablespoons olive oil

1½ teaspoons dried thyme (or substitute 5 sprigs fresh thyme)

Salt and freshly ground pepper

2 tablespoons sweet vermouth

Fresh parsley, to garnish

Bring the stock, water, ham hocks, and bay leaf to a boil over high heat in a large saucepan. Reduce to a simmer. Cook together for 1 hour, or until the hocks are tender.

Heat the butter and oil together in a large sauté pan over medium-high heat. When bubbling, add the onion. Reduce heat to medium and then cook for 5 minutes, or until the onion has just softened. Add the cabbage, stir to coat, season with thyme, salt, and pepper and cook until wilted, about 10 minutes; set aside.

After the stock has finished simmering, remove the ham hocks and bay leaf. Set them aside. When the hocks are cool enough to handle, trim out any lean, pink flesh, cut thinly, and set aside. Pour the cabbage mixture and trimmed pork flesh into the stock, bring to a boil, reduce to a simmer, and cook about 30 minutes, or until very tender. Add the vermouth, verify seasoning, and continue cooking for another 8 minutes. If you've used fresh thyme sprigs, be sure to remove the tough stalks at this point. Garnish with a sprinkle of finely chopped fresh parsley and serve immediately.

Serves 8

JULIENNE KNOW-HOW

Julienne is a pretty French word (pronounced joo-lee-EHN) that sounds far more foreign and complicated than its practical function and simple realization. It is a helpful cutting skill to put to use in your kitchen when working with everything from potatoes to greens. The technique yields thin, even-sized strips of vegetables (and more), which increases the aesthetic appeal of many foods and also ensures even cooking time.

In preparing a julienne, the product you're working with is stacked in manageable piles, the uneven edges are cut away and discarded, and the product is then cut into approximately ⅛-inch-wide strips, working your chef's knife through the horizontal length of the stack. To julienne a rounded, thicker vegetable such as a carrot or a potato, there are two additional steps. First, trim the rounded edges slightly so the vegetable will lie flush and flat on the cutting board. Then, using a chef's knife, cut through the vegetable lengthwise to create several ⅛-inch-thick planks. Finally, stack the planks and cut through these from the top of the stack to create ⅛-inch-wide batons.

Once you get the hang of it, you'll find that "julienning" is much more fun and practical than pulling out a food processor to cut a bunch of vegetables, and you'll probably do a better job—provided your knife is sharp.

FRESH SWEET ONION AND CORN CHOWDER

One of the things I get most excited about in spring are the pearly white bulbs of sweet onions with their crowns of grass-green stems. Pulled fresh from the just-warmed earth, they ooze a spring freshness that belies the dormancy of winter through which they've grown while the rest of us have slept. In this delicate, sweet chowder, onion flavor is layered throughout. Though the corn at markets this time of year comes primarily from Florida, it is usually very fresh and sweet. Look for the Silver Queen variety. Its crunchy texture pops with each creamy bite.

1 tablespoon olive oil

1 tablespoon butter

¾ cup cubed pancetta (or bacon), cut into ¼-inch cubes

3 medium fresh sweet onions, trimmed, halved, and thinly sliced (reserve the green stems from 1 of the onions to garnish)

Salt and freshly ground pepper

1 to 2 tablespoons finely chopped fresh thyme

2 tablespoons sweet or dry vermouth

¼ cup dry white wine

4 cups chicken stock

2 cups fresh corn, cut from the cob (about 2 to 3 ears corn)

1 to 2 tablespoons half-and-half

1 tablespoon butter (optional)

Heat the oil and 1 tablespoon butter together in a large saucepan over medium-high heat. Add the pancetta and toss to coat. Cook, stirring, about 5 minutes, or until lightly browned on all sides. Add the onions and stir to coat. Season generously with salt and pepper. Reduce heat to medium. Cook until softened, stirring from time to time, about 12 minutes. Add the thyme, vermouth, and wine. Bring to a boil and reduce heat to medium. Cook until the liquid has reduced by half, and then add the stock and corn. Bring to a boil and reduce to a simmer. Cook until corn has softened, about 15 minutes more. Add the half-and-half and remaining butter. Taste and adjust seasoning if necessary. Serve with a sprinkle of freshly cut thyme and some of the reserved onion greens, lightly chopped.

Serves 4–6

COOL DILL AND CURRY-SPIKED CUCUMBER SOUP

Completely heat- and cooking-free, this refreshing soup gets nods from Indian and Greek cooking cultures using the coolest vegetable of the hot months: the cucumber. Though I'm not normally a fan of cold soups, this low-calorie delight soothes and satisfies when temperatures soar. Use any leftovers as a topping for baked potatoes or a dressing for a cool potato salad.

2 cups low-fat plain yogurt

½ cup whipping cream

2 large cucumbers, peeled, seeded, and grated

2 cloves garlic, minced

2 teaspoons white wine vinegar

Juice of ½ lime

2 to 3 tablespoons good-quality olive oil

¼ cup low-sodium or homemade chicken stock

¼ cup finely chopped fresh dill

1 teaspoon ground curry

Salt and freshly ground pepper

Sprig of fresh dill, to garnish (optional)

Curry, to garnish (optional)

Gently combine the yogurt, cream, and cucumbers in a medium bowl. Stir in all the remaining ingredients except garnishes. Add more stock if the soup seems too thick. Chill 1 to 3 hours, covered, before serving. Garnish with a sprig of fresh dill and a light dusting of curry, if desired.

NOTE: Refrigerated, this soup stores reasonably well. However, you will want to eat it before 2 days have passed or the cucumbers may become soggy.

Serves 4–6

SWEET CORN AND CROWDER PEA CHOWDER

Corn and crowder peas, a Southern field pea so named because the seeds are densely crowded together in the pod, hit the markets in unison and are on from the early days of summer through the autumnal call of Labor Day.

Silver Queen corn, a hybrid, is one of several sweet corn varieties (which range in color and sugar levels) that run deliciously rampant in the heat of Southern summers. In this delicate soup, the naked cobs simmer in fresh water, providing an initial layer of flavor that is reinforced with pop-in-your-mouth-fresh nuggets of corn and the earthy girth and texture of pretty, brick-red crowder peas.

6 ears Silver Queen (or another sweet variety) corn, husked and rinsed

4 slices bacon, cut into 1/4-inch dice

1 tablespoon bacon fat

3 tablespoons butter, divided

1 medium-size onion, finely diced

1 tablespoon flour

6 cups strained corn stock

2 cups diced fingerling potatoes (or another fresh, waxy variety), cleaned and cut into 1/4-inch dice with skin on

2 cups fresh crowder peas, well-rinsed

Salt and freshly ground pepper

2 tablespoons dry vermouth

1/4 cup whole cream

1/4 teaspoon truffle oil or extra virgin olive oil (optional)

Chopped fresh parsley, to garnish

Using a long knife with a serrated edge, cut the corn away from the cob. (**NOTE**: Try holding the cob upright and cut down. Making a bed of a couple of clean kitchen towels helps to keep the corn from flying everywhere.) Reserve the freshly cut corn, which should yield about 3 cups. Place the cobs in a large pot, covered by about 6 cups cold water, lightly salted. Bring to a boil and reduce to a simmer; cook about 20 minutes. Strain the stock and set aside, discarding the corn cobs.

Separately, brown the bacon over medium-high heat in a large soup pot. Cook until crisp, stirring, about 5 minutes. Remove bacon from the pan and set aside to drain on paper towels. Discard all but 1 tablespoon of the bacon fat. Add 1 tablespoon butter to the pot and heat over medium. Add the onion and cook gently, stirring, about 5 minutes, or until translucent but not browned. Add the flour, stir, and cook 5 minutes more over medium heat. Increase the heat to high and add the reserved corn stock. Stir vigorously with a wooden spoon to scrape up any brown bits on the bottom of the pot. Reduce to a simmer. Add the corn, potatoes, peas, salt, and pepper. Bring to a boil and reduce to a simmer. Cook until corn, peas, and potatoes are tender—about 45 minutes. Just before serving, add the reserved cooked bacon, vermouth, remaining butter, cream, and oil and cook through for another 10 minutes, or until hot. Garnish with the parsley and serve.

Serves 8–10

CURRIED TOMATO AND OKRA STEW

Favored Southern seasonal twins, okra and tomatoes come together with a pinch of curry in this chunky stew. Serve over rice for a satisfying vegetarian meal. The tomatoes must be peeled to ensure a silky texture. To do so, cut out the stem at the top of the tomato and carve out a small "X" across the top with your knife-tip. Prepare a pot of boiling water and submerge the tomatoes for about 30 seconds. Chill under cold running water and the skin will peel right off. You can do the same thing with peaches, by the way.

3 to 4 tablespoons olive oil

1 medium onion, finely chopped

3 cloves garlic, minced

2 tablespoons curry powder (or to taste)

Salt and freshly ground pepper

3 cups sliced fresh okra

3 tomatoes, peeled and coarsely chopped

¾ cup water or chicken stock

Pinch of sugar, if desired (this depends on the sweetness of the tomatoes, and your taste buds)

¼ cup chopped fresh parsley

Heat the oil in a large skillet over medium-high heat. Add the onion, garlic, and seasonings; stir. Reduce heat to medium and cook until soft, about 5 minutes. Add the okra and sauté 5 minutes. Add the tomatoes, water, and sugar. Cook until tender, about 30 minutes. Taste and adjust accordingly. Stir in the fresh parsley. Serve warm over rice or grits, or as is with a fat wedge of cornbread.

Serves 6

FRESH BUTTER BEAN AND SMOKED HAM HOCK SOUP

Pork and beans come together in cultures across the world, but in this soup, distinctly Southern butter beans and the South's revered pig merge dreamily together in decidedly Southern elegance that costs only pennies to make.

1 tablespoon butter

1 onion, finely chopped

1 celery stalk, finely chopped

1 clove garlic, smashed

Salt and freshly ground pepper

1 ham hock (smoked pig's knuckle)

3 cups fresh butter beans

3 tablespoons extra dry vermouth

3 cups chicken stock

Pinch of red pepper flakes

2 cups water

1/2 cup half-and-half

3 tablespoons finely chopped fresh parsley

3 green onions, finely chopped

In a large pot, melt the butter over medium heat. Add the onion, celery, garlic, salt, and pepper, and cook until softened, stirring occasionally. About 4 minutes later, add the ham hock, coat with the butter, and cook 3 minutes more. Add the butter beans, vermouth, stock, red pepper flakes, and water. Bring to a boil, reduce to a simmer over low heat, and cook until the beans are very soft and the soup has reduced, about 45 minutes to 1 hour.

To finish the soup, remove the ham hock and set aside until cool enough to handle. Trim off the exterior layer of fat and cut out any shards of smoked meat, discarding the fat. Cut the ham into a small, uniform dice and set aside. Meanwhile, puree the soup in a food processor or blender until frothy and smooth. Return the soup to the cooking pot and add the reserved ham. Bring to a simmer over high heat and then reduce heat to simmer. Finish with the half-and-half and fresh parsley. Taste and adjust seasonings as needed. Serve immediately and top with a dusting of green onions.

NOTE: This soup can be made ahead of time, minus the half-and-half, and refrigerated for a day or two or frozen for a few months. Reheat and finish with half-and-half, seasonings as needed, and garnish to serve.

Serves 6–8

MEATY AND MEATLESS WILD MUSHROOM SOUP

One chilly Thanksgiving morning with the daunting specter of soon-to-arrive guests swirling through my mind, I spied a bin, pregnant with awe-inspiring clusters of silky, pale gray oyster mushrooms. The mushroom scene and the nervous-hostess timing of it all inspired the recipe for this meaty, meatless soup. Vegetarians have long exalted mushrooms for their nutrition, meaty texture, and subtle earthy flavors. I've loved them ever since I found two French pals, who would regularly pick fresh-from-the-forest cèpes (aka porcini) from the woods surrounding their home. On especially lucky days, they would call me and invite me over to share a simple cèpe omelet made with farm-fresh eggs and a "coup" of Blanquette de Limoux, a sparkling wine from the region. Pure, unsolicited bliss, indeed!

This recipe wastes nothing, as the tough stems or "feet" from the mushrooms are used to prepare the stock that becomes the base for the soup. This is a show stopper of a first course for Thanksgiving dinner.

FOR THE MUSHROOM STOCK

1 tablespoon olive oil
1 tablespoon butter
1 onion, peeled and finely diced
1 carrot, peeled and finely diced
1 stalk celery, finely diced
"Feet" from each of the
    following mushrooms:
    4 cups coarsely chopped
    fresh oyster mushrooms,
    2 cups sliced fresh shiitake
    mushrooms, 4 cups coarsely
    chopped fresh portobello
    mushrooms
Salt and freshly ground pepper
3 tablespoons dry vermouth
10 cups water
8 sprigs fresh parsley, bound in
    kitchen string

To prepare the stock, heat the oil and butter together in a stockpot over medium heat. Add the onion, carrot, and celery and cook or "sweat" gently, about 5 minutes, or until the vegetables release their juices and soften. While that's going on, trim the very base of the mushrooms and discard. Wipe down the mushrooms—do not rinse or submerge in water—with a paper towel to remove any dirt. Gently pull the feet off the caps of all the mushrooms and chop coarsely; reserve the caps for later. Add the mushroom feet to the pot and stir to coat; season with salt and pepper. Continue cooking over medium heat until softened, about 3 minutes. Add the dry vermouth, increase the heat to high, and cook down to a glaze. Add the water and parsley bundle, bring the stock to a boil and reduce to a simmer; cook for 20 to 25 minutes. Strain through a fine strainer or chinois and reserve the stock, discarding the solids.

FOR THE SOUP

2 tablespoons butter

2 tablespoons olive oil

4 leeks, trimmed, and cut into
an even, fine dice

I shallot, finely diced

3 cloves garlic, minced

Salt and freshly ground pepper

Reserved oyster, shiitake, and
portobello mushroom caps,
finely sliced

½ cup sweet vermouth

I tablespoon porcini oil
(optional)

6 cups prepared mushroom
stock

I teaspoon herbs de Provence

I cup whole cream

I to 2 tablespoons butter
(optional)

To prepare the soup, melt together the butter and oil in a large pot over medium-high heat. Add the leeks, shallot, garlic, salt, and pepper. Cook, stirring until the vegetables have softened, about 5 minutes. Add the sliced/chopped mushroom caps, stir, and cook until softened. Increase the heat to high and add the vermouth. Cook down to a glaze and add the porcini oil, stock, and herbs de Provence. (**NOTE**: Any remaining stock can be refrigerated or frozen for use at a later date.) Bring to a boil and simmer together for about 20 minutes, or until the flavors are well developed. Taste and adjust seasonings. Just before serving, add the cream and butter, if desired. Stir until heated through and serve immediately. Garnish with finely chopped fresh parsley or thyme.

Serves 6–8

BUTTERCUP SQUASH SOUP
WITH FRIED BASIL LEAVES

For a while, heirloom variety winter squash, such as the lovely, sweet buttercup used in this soup, fell out of favor in part because the steel talons of modern machinery found their unusual, oblong shapes difficult to harvest. Now, lesser known heirlooms with charming names such as sweet dumpling, Golden Nugget, Hubbard, Turban, and Long Island Cheese Squash are coming to the fore because smaller farmers are making the effort to give these squash another chance and because smart farmers-market buyers are asking for them. Buttercup is a heavy, turban-shaped squash with a dense, sweet potato–like flesh. Like most winter squash, it can be roasted, baked, pureed, and folded into soups, quick breads, pies, and cakes.

FOR THE SOUP

1 medium buttercup squash, halved and seeded

1 medium onion, peeled and finely diced

2 stalks celery, finely diced

1 tablespoon olive oil

Salt and freshly ground pepper

4 cups chicken stock

Dash of ground ginger

Dash of ground cinnamon

About 1 teaspoon local honey (depending on sweetness of the squash)

1/2 cup half-and-half or whole cream

FOR THE FRIED BASIL

1/4 cup vegetable or canola oil

Fresh basil leaves

To prepare the soup, preheat oven to 400 degrees. Place the squash cut side down on a roasting pan. Roast on the center rack until tender, about 40 to 50 minutes; set aside to cool.

Meanwhile, sauté the onion and celery in oil in a medium-size pot over medium-high heat until translucent, about 5 minutes. Season the mixture lightly with salt and pepper. Add the chicken stock, ginger, cinnamon, and honey (as needed). Bring to a boil and reduce to a simmer, cooking together for about 10 minutes; set aside. Once the squash is cool enough to handle, peel off the skin or scoop out the cooked flesh. Discard the rind and add the cooked flesh to the stock mixture. Puree with a handheld processor or in the bowl of a food processor until smooth. Return the soup to the pot. Bring to a boil and reduce to a simmer. Season to taste with salt and pepper. Just before serving, add cream and cook through until warm.

To prepare the fried basil, heat the oil in a shallow skillet over medium-high heat. When bubbling, reduce to medium. Add the leaves in batches of two. Cook about 30 seconds on each side—it will snap, crackle, and pop to tell you it's cooking—and drain on paper towels. Garnish each bowl of hot soup with 3 or 4 leaves.

Serves 4–6

RICH ROASTED PUMPKIN SOUP
WITH FANCY SPICED CROUTONS

When I apprenticed at Fauchon's Le 30 Restaurant off sexy Place de la Madeleine in Paris,
this sophisticated take on pumpkin soup was a standard fall dish. In this variation (fresh
pie pumpkin can be substituted with another deep orange winter squash like buttercup
or butternut), the squash is braised in milk and stock, gaining additional flavor from
aromatic vegetables, curry, and allspice. The soup is topped off with petite croutons laced
with butter and allspice, giving depth and texture to this holiday-perfect soup.

FOR THE SOUP

1 small pie pumpkin (about 4
    pounds), peeled and cut into
    2-inch cubes
1 medium onion, peeled and
    quartered
1 medium carrot, peeled and
    cut into 2-inch-thick rounds
2 cups chicken stock
2 cups whole milk
Pinch of curry
Dash of allspice
Salt and freshly ground pepper
1 tablespoon local honey
1/2 cup whole cream

FOR THE CROUTONS

3 tablespoons butter
1 cup cubed baguette bread
    (cut into 1/4-inch cubes)
1 tablespoon allspice
Salt and freshly ground pepper
1/2 teaspoon light brown sugar

Fresh chives, chopped

To prepare the soup, preheat the oven to 425 degrees. Cut the pumpkin in half, then remove and discard seeds and pulp. Next, cut the pumpkin "sides" into 2-inch wedges, peel and cut into 2-inch cubes. Place in a sturdy roasting pan with the remaining soup ingredients, except the cream. Cover tightly with aluminum foil and cook until the pumpkin and vegetables are tender, about 1 hour and 15 minutes.

Meanwhile, prepare the croutons. Melt the butter over medium-high heat in a large sauté pan; add the bread cubes and sprinkle with seasonings. Cook, tossing occasionally, until golden on all sides. Sprinkle with brown sugar, toss, and cook another few seconds. Remove from the heat and cool on paper towels.

Once the soup mixture has cooked and cooled slightly, ladle the soup in batches into a food processor (or process with a handheld mixer) and blend until silky smooth. For added silkiness, strain the soup through a fine sieve or chinois to remove any errant chunks.

To serve, bring soup to a boil, then reduce heat to a simmer. Add cream and adjust seasonings if necessary. Heat thoroughly and serve individually. Top each serving with several croutons and a sprinkling of fresh chives.

NOTE: The soup base and the croutons can be prepared 1 to 2 days in advance. Only add the cream when reheating, however. Store croutons in an airtight container and reheat in a warm oven to give them renewed "crisp."

Serves 6

HEARTY SAUSAGE
AND NORTHERN BEAN SOUP WITH KALE

If you get your hands on some fine artisanal sausage and a fresh bunch of kale, bring it together with some dried beans (substitute navy or lima beans if desired) from your farmers market pantry for this satisfying, Tuscan-inspired meal in a bowl. You can cut cooking time way down by using canned beans, but I prefer the texture of dried beans. If you decide to go with canned, drain them very well and add them at the end of cooking so that they heat through but don't break down to mush in the process.

1½ cups dried great Northern beans

3 sprigs fresh rosemary

1 tablespoon salt

1 tablespoon olive oil

6 links sweet Italian sausage (or substitute another artisanal sausage), sliced into ½-inch-thick pieces

Salt and freshly ground pepper

1 onion, peeled and diced

4 cloves garlic, peeled and mashed

3 tablespoons white wine

4 cups chicken stock

4 cups water

2 tomatoes, coarsely chopped

Dash of red pepper flakes

2 teaspoons herbs de Provence or chopped fresh rosemary

Dash of balsamic vinegar

½ cup orecchiette pasta (or substitute macaroni)

1 large bunch fresh kale, all tough stalks removed and cut into thin strips

Grated aged Italian cheese (optional)

Rinse and drain the beans. Place in a pot and cover generously with cold water. Add the rosemary sprigs; bring to a boil and reduce to a simmer. Cook until crisp-tender, about 45 minutes. Add the tablespoon of salt halfway through the cooking; drain well. Remove rosemary sprigs and set aside.

Meanwhile, heat the oil over medium-high heat for 1 to 2 minutes in a large, sturdy soup pot or Dutch oven. Add the sausage and brown well, stirring from time to time. This should take about 5 minutes. Season to taste with salt and pepper. Remove the sausage from the pot with a slotted spoon and set aside.

Drain off all but 2 tablespoons of fat from the sausage; add the onion and garlic. Season with more salt and pepper and cook over medium heat, stirring until softened, about 5 minutes. Add the wine. Stir up any brown bits on the bottom and reduce the wine by half, about 2 minutes. Add the stock, water, tomatoes, reserved beans, and reserved sausage. Bring to a boil and reduce to a moderate simmer. Cook for about 5 minutes. Add more salt, pepper, red pepper flakes, herbs de Provence, vinegar, and pasta. Cook until the pasta is al dente, about 10 minutes (depending on the type of pasta you use). Finish with the kale, stirring it into the soup until just wilted, about 2 minutes. Taste and adjust seasonings if needed. Serve immediately with grated aged Italian cheese, if desired.

Serves 10–12

CREAMY WHITE TURNIP SOUP
WITH SPRING ONIONS AND ROASTED GARLIC

By all means, give these creamy white turnip orbs (some varieties come with a pretty purple blush) a try. Pulled fresh from the ground, an increasing army of turnip hybrids available at farmers markets are light years away from the pungent, tough, waxy, long-stored turnips that formerly gave turnips an unglamorous reputation.

This soup is delicately feminine, ever so elegant and one of my personal favorites. The salty bite of prosciutto nicely counters the sweetness of the onions and turnips. Save the turnip greens for a quick sauté in olive oil with a bit of garlic and serve it alongside.

1 head roasted garlic

1 bunch (about 4 cups) white turnips, trimmed, peeled (outer layer discarded), and cut into 2-inch cubes

1 medium spring onion, root and green top trimmed to 1-inch lengths from the bulb and cut into 8 wedges

4 cups low-sodium chicken stock

Salt and freshly ground pepper

1/4 teaspoon ground nutmeg

2 slices prosciutto, cut into thin strips and 1-inch lengths

1/4 cup crème fraîche or whole cream

Green onion tops, to garnish

Preheat oven to 425 degrees. Trim the top of the garlic and wrap with foil. Place in the middle of the oven and roast until soft to the touch, about 30 to 45 minutes. When the garlic is cool enough to handle, squeeze out the soft pulp by pressing the blade of a chef's knife against the bulb to release the roasted flesh; discard the papery casings.

Place the garlic, turnips, onions, and chicken stock in a large saucepan. Season lightly with salt and pepper. Bring to a boil and then reduce to a simmer. Cook, uncovered, until the turnips are tender, about 30 to 45 minutes. Remove from the stove and puree until smooth with a handheld blender or food processor. Return the soup to the pan. Add the nutmeg, prosciutto, and crème fraîche. Bring to a boil and reduce to a simmer, stirring to blend. Taste and adjust seasonings as required. Garnish with a sprinkling of freshly chopped green onions and serve immediately.

NOTE: This soup can be prepared in advance and frozen or stored in the refrigerator. However, if you plan to do so, add the cream just before serving, not before storing.

Serves 4–6

SUMPTUOUS SALADS AND STELLAR SIDES

MOTHER'S MULTICOLORED
ROASTED BEET AND WHITE ONION SALAD

Managing four children, running all over God's creation, and overseeing more pets than Noah's Ark's passenger list wasn't easy for my mother. So, though she always cooked us solid, nutritious meals, she didn't spend a lot of time on or pay much attention to detail in the kitchen. However, after the chicks finally left her nest, she found time to kick her cooking skill and interest in cooking into high gear.

This fabulous salad is similar to something she put together for a family feast a few years ago, after she'd found her inner gourmet. It's elevated further with the sweetness of roasted, fresh beets as opposed to the flavorless canned variety. Fresh beets can be found at farmers markets in a rainbow of colors—orange, red, and pink—and they make this salad as colorful as it is delicious.

6 medium raw beets (choose from assorted colors), scrubbed and tops removed

2 tablespoons olive oil

Salt and freshly ground pepper

1 medium white onion (or Vidalia)

FOR THE VINAIGRETTE

3 tablespoons aged red wine vinegar

1 tablespoon Dijon mustard

1 teaspoon local honey

2 cloves garlic, mashed

1 teaspoon chopped fresh thyme leaves

4 to 6 tablespoons extra virgin olive oil

Salt and freshly ground pepper

Fresh cilantro leaves, to garnish

Preheat oven to 425 degrees. Arrange the whole, trimmed beets in a roasting pan, tossing with the oil, salt, and pepper. Roast for about 1 hour, or until tender when pierced with a fork. Remove from the oven and set aside to cool. Meanwhile, peel and thinly slice the onion, and then set aside.

To prepare the vinaigrette, whisk together the vinegar, mustard, honey, garlic, and thyme in a medium bowl. Gradually incorporate the oil in a thin stream, whisking constantly to emulsify. Season to taste with salt and pepper. Add the onions to the vinaigrette, tossing to coat. Cover, and set aside at room temperature for up to 2 hours (or refrigerate overnight, covered, and bring to room temperature before serving).

Once the beets have been cooked, trim outer skin and cut into ⅛-inch-thick slices. If using different colored beets, keep them separate to prevent bleeding. Refrigerate, covered, until ready to use. **NOTE:** The beets can be prepared and stored for up to 3 days.

To assemble, arrange a bed of onions in the center of each plate using a slotted spoon to drain off any excess vinaigrette. Arrange several slices of beets next to or over the onions. Top with a few fresh cilantro leaves and a light drizzle of leftover vinaigrette. Season with more freshly ground pepper and serve.

Serves 4–6

WILD HONEY–GLAZED CARROTS
WITH MINT AND GREEN ONIONS

The French are fond of blending carrots and pearl onions in a pan and cooking them down to a glaze of reduced water, sugar, and butter. This combination is frequently served as a side dish or tops off a big pot of braised stew; classically, a boeuf bourguignonne. You can do the same with this variation on the theme, but go ahead and use wild, local honey instead of sugar. The flavor layers are so much more interesting and vary with the season, depending on what's flowering. Mint is a fun addition (but not a requirement) that invites an accompanying platter of lamb chops or leg of lamb.

1 pound baby carrots, whole, or fresh carrots, peeled and cut into ½-inch-thick rounds

Salt and freshly ground pepper

2 tablespoons butter

2 green onions or the green tops of 2 spring onions (when in season)

2 tablespoons julienned fresh mint

1 to 2 tablespoons wild honey

Place the carrots in a large, shallow skillet and cover halfway with water. Season to taste with salt and pepper, and then add the butter. Bring to a boil over high heat; reduce heat to low and cover. Cook until the carrots are fork tender, about 20 to 25 minutes. Remove the lid and increase the heat to high. Cook until the water has reduced down to about 3 tablespoons.

Add the green onion tops, mint, and honey. Cook together until warmed through, about 30 seconds. Season to taste and serve immediately.

Serves 4–6

ZESTY SAUTÉED LACINATO KALE WITH GARLIC

Greens are gold in the South, where they're thought to bring good fortune. Almost any semi-sturdy green, including Swiss chard, beet greens, mustard greens, and tat soi, will stand up to a quick, hot sauté to wilt the greens in a matter of minutes, sealing in their gorgeous color, healthy nutrients, and mild, tart flavor. Lacinato kale, also known as Tuscan kale, dinosaur kale, or Italian heirloom kale, is a curly, crunchy variety of the green that does especially well cooked simply and quickly, as in this recipe.

2 large bunches lacinato kale,
    stems and ribs removed
2 tablespoons olive oil
3 cloves garlic, minced
Salt and freshly ground pepper
Splash of red wine vinegar
1 teaspoon fresh orange zest

Chop the kale into 2-inch squares. Heat a large, deep skillet over medium-high heat. Add the oil and heat through until just starting to move in the pan. Add the garlic and sear quickly, coloring to a pale golden color, but do not brown or char. Add the greens and toss to coat; season to taste with salt and pepper. Cook together, tossing occasionally, for 2 to 3 minutes, or until the kale has just wilted and is tender. Drizzle with the vinegar and add the orange zest. Toss together and serve immediately.

Serves 4

KALE CEVICHE

This snappy, fresh recipe comes from the kitchen of Sarah Blacklin, market manager at the Carrboro Farmers Market in charming Carrboro, North Carolina. As with a seafood ceviche, the kale is cooked by the acid of the lemon juice. Sarah suggests adding a little fish sauce to the salad for a saltier edge.

3 to 4 bunches fresh kale
1/2 medium onion, finely
    chopped or sliced into
    a julienne (optional)
Juice from 2 medium lemons
1/4 teaspoon cayenne
1/4 cup extra virgin olive oil
Salt and freshly ground pepper

Rinse the kale and tear into bite-size pieces, making sure to remove the tough stems. Place the kale and onion in a large salad bowl. Pour lemon juice over top and toss thoroughly, coating all the leaves. Add the cayenne, oil, salt, and pepper. Toss together well, cover, and refrigerate overnight. This will give the acidity enough time to "sink" into the kale and soften it before eating.

Serves 6–8

HOW SWEET IT IS
GRILLED ONION SALAD

Fresh, sweet onions of early spring are so magnificent they're "tear" inspiring. Happily, their low sulfur content and high sugar content translate to limited cry-time when you're working with them—just one of their many glories. Milky white, they crunch like an apple and are mild enough to eat raw. Grilling is one of the best ways to bring out their goodness, but if your grill is on the fritz or you don't feel like the fuss, the onions brown nicely under a broiler as well.

FOR THE VINAIGRETTE

¼ cup fresh orange juice

1 tablespoon Dijon mustard

3 cloves garlic, crushed

1 tablespoon red wine vinegar

1 teaspoon local honey

3 tablespoons finely sliced onion greens (from the fresh onion tops)

1 to 2 tablespoons extra virgin olive oil

Salt and freshly ground pepper

FOR THE ONIONS

2 large, fresh sweet onions, peeled and cut into ½-inch-thick slabs

¼ cup extra virgin olive oil

Salt and freshly ground pepper

FOR THE SALAD

4 cups mesclun greens or spring mix

A couple of hours before serving, prepare the vinaigrette. Combine all but the oil, salt, and pepper in a small bowl and whisk to combine. Slowly, drizzle in the oil while whisking. Season with salt and pepper to taste. Cover and set aside at room temperature for 1 to 2 hours.

To prepare the onions, preheat the outdoor grill or broiler. Place the onion slices on the grill or broiler pan. Brush lightly with oil and season with salt and pepper. Grill or broil until slightly soft and charred to a golden brown—about 5 minutes over medium heat. Turn, brush with more oil, and season with salt and pepper; grill about 5 minutes more.

Remove the onions from the heat and place in a small bowl. When cool enough to handle, gently break up the rings. Toss lightly with the vinaigrette (you will have a little left over). Season if necessary. Arrange on a bed of greens, drizzled lightly and tossed with the remaining vinaigrette, on a serving platter or individual plates. Serve immediately, while the onions are still warm.

Serves 4–6

SWISS RAINBOW CHARD SALAD
WITH BLACK-EYED PEA SLAW

You'd have to be luckier than a leprechaun to find fresh black-eyed peas and greens on the same day at farmers markets since greens' cool weather growing season window closes just about the time field peas' hot weather growing season window opens.

Since most greens are highly perishable, go for fresh, local rainbow chard and substitute fresh black-eyed peas with canned or frozen.

1 bunch Swiss rainbow chard, rinsed and trimmed

FOR THE SLAW

1 (15-ounce) can black-eyed peas, drained and rinsed
1/2 poblano pepper, seeded and finely diced
1/2 red onion, finely diced
2 cloves garlic, mashed
2 tablespoons finely chopped fresh sage
2 tablespoons finely chopped fresh parsley
2 tablespoons fresh-squeezed orange juice
1 tablespoon good-quality extra virgin olive oil
3 slices prosciutto, finely diced
Dash of balsamic vinegar
Salt and freshly ground pepper

FOR THE VINAIGRETTE

2 1/2 tablespoons port vinegar or balsamic vinegar
1 clove garlic, mashed
1 tablespoon Dijon mustard
4 tablespoons good-quality extra virgin olive oil
Salt and freshly ground pepper

Wash, trim and cut the chard into 1/8-inch-thick strips (see Julienne Know-How, page 37). Dry thoroughly by rolling gently in two or three clean kitchen towels. Refrigerate, wrapped loosely in a damp kitchen towel.

To prepare the slaw, gently combine all of the ingredients in a medium-size bowl and season with salt and pepper to taste. Cover and set aside at room temperature for at least 1 hour to allow the flavors to mature.

To prepare the vinaigrette, whisk together the vinegar, garlic, and mustard in a small bowl. Gradually whisk in the oil; season with salt and pepper to taste.

The salad can be presented on a large platter or plated individually. Either way, toss the greens in a light coating of the vinaigrette. Season with salt and pepper. Build a large, airy mound of dressed greens. Top with equal portions of slaw, and then serve at room temperature.

Serves 4

CHRISTMAS
COLLARDS

A generous pinch of allspice and everything nice puts a festive finish on what is arguably the South's most celebrated green. A splash of red wine vinegar near the very end of the collard's slow, tenderness-inducing braise makes this a lip-smackingly delicious side dish.

2 large heads collards, stems
    removed
2 tablespoons olive oil
1 (1-inch-thick) slab salt pork
1 small onion, halved and thinly
    sliced
Generous pinch of allspice
Salt and freshly ground pepper
1 cup chicken stock
1 1/2 tablespoons red wine
    vinegar

Rinse the collards thoroughly and then cut out the tough central stem. Stack the leaves in small piles and slice the collards into 1-inch squares. Meanwhile, heat the oil and salt pork in a large, sturdy pot over medium-high heat. Add the onion and sauté until tender, about 3 minutes. Add the greens, allspice, salt, pepper, and stock. Cover and cook over medium-low heat, stirring occasionally, until the greens are very tender, about 45 minutes.

Just before serving, add the vinegar and heat through. Taste and adjust seasonings if necessary. Remove ham and salt pork and discard, or, if desired, slice the pork and stir it into the dish. Serve immediately.

Serves 4–6

COLLARD
GREENS
picked yesturday!

FRESH TURNIP, APPLE, AND RED ONION SLAW

Here's another refreshing take on slaw, this one putting fresh-from-the-ground sweet turnips into flavor and texture play. The raw crunch of turnips is lovely with apples and happens to pair particularly well with the sweet and tart flavor of the heirloom McIntosh apple. Red onion adds color and bite. A light vinaigrette of lemon juice and olive oil infused with fresh thyme tastes just like spring and is all this beautiful, fresh-tasting salad needs to bring it together.

1 head Bibb lettuce, core removed and leaves separated

1 McIntosh apple, cored and cut into 1/4-inch-long strips, skin-on

3 turnips, ends trimmed and cut into 1/4-inch-long strips

1/2 medium red onion, trimmed, peeled and cut into 1/4-inch-long strips

Juice of 1 lemon

3 to 4 tablespoons extra virgin olive oil

1 tablespoon local honey

Salt and freshly ground pepper

2 tablespoons chopped fresh thyme

1/2 cup chopped walnuts

Several sprigs fresh thyme

Set aside 8 of the larger attractive green leaves of Bibb lettuce. Stack and gently roll the remaining leaves into a cigar-like shape and cut into thin strips. Place the chopped lettuce in a bowl with the remaining ingredients except the walnuts and thyme and toss thoroughly. Taste and adjust seasoning as required. To plate, arrange two of the large leaves on a salad plate to form a bed. Place a generous mound (about 3/4 cup) of the salad in the center. Garnish with a sprig or two of fresh thyme and a handful of walnuts. Serve immediately.

NOTE: The mixed salad can be prepared and chilled for up to 2 hours ahead of service. It needs to be tossed at the time it is prepared, however, since the lemon juice prevents the apple from discoloring.

Serves 4

SPINACH AND RADISH SALAD
WITH CANDIED PECANS AND RED WINE VINAIGRETTE

The buttery roundness of spinach, the peppery crunch of fresh radishes, and a sweet dose of candied pecans celebrate the cooler temperatures of early spring and fall with colorful aplomb in this festive salad.

FOR THE VINAIGRETTE

1 shallot, finely diced
4 tablespoons red wine vinegar
1 tablespoon local honey
1 tablespoon Dijon mustard
Salt and freshly ground pepper
¼ cup good-quality virgin
    olive oil

FOR THE CANDIED NUTS

1 tablespoon olive oil
1 tablespoon butter
1 cup coarsely chopped pecans
Salt and freshly ground pepper
2 tablespoons brown sugar

FOR THE SALAD

6 cups fresh spinach, cleaned
    and rough stems removed
20 radishes, cleaned, trimmed,
    and quartered lengthwise
Salt and freshly ground pepper

To prepare the vinaigrette, combine the shallot, vinegar, honey, mustard, salt, and pepper in a small bowl. Whisk thoroughly to combine. Gradually drizzle in the oil, whisking constantly. Taste to verify seasonings. Cover and set aside 1 hour at room temperature.

Meanwhile, prepare the nuts. Heat a medium-size sauté pan over medium-high heat. Add the oil and butter. When bubbling, add the pecans, salt, and pepper; toss to coat. Continue tossing until golden, about 2 minutes. Add the sugar, continuing to toss. Reduce heat to medium. Cook until the sugar has caramelized to a dark, golden color. Remove from heat and drain on paper towels; cool.

To prepare the salad, toss the spinach with the radishes. Add the vinaigrette and toss to coat. Season the salad with salt and pepper. Arrange on individual plates or a single platter and sprinkle with candied nuts. Serve immediately.

Serves 4

VINAIGRETTE: THE MOTHER OF ALL SAUCES

One of the four "mother sauces" of classical cuisine, a vinaigrette is by far the easiest and most versatile of them all. In its simplest form, a vinaigrette combines oil and vinegar with a little seasoning and is used to dress salads and can also function as a marinade or dressing for meats, poultry, or fish. The ratio of oil to vinegar depends on your taste, but the standard ratio is generally accepted to be one part vinegar to three parts oil. The goal is to get a mini-reflex in the back of your throat and tongue that wakes up the palate for the meal that's coming.

With the endless list of new oils and vinegars available today, and the utter simplicity of preparing your own signature vinaigrettes, it seems insane to purchase a chemically laden, emulsifier-drenched bottled variety. Mix it up, have some fun, and save yourself some money while you're at it.

I almost always use some Dijon mustard and some local honey as the base to any vinaigrette I make because both give big-time flavor and are natural emulsifiers. A flavor shot of shallots, garlic, or fresh herbs is nice, too. The good news is, if you're looking to reduce fat in your life, starting with a lower-level acid base (such as fresh orange juice instead of red wine vinegar) in your vinaigrette will mean you'll need to add very little oil to "round" out the acid flavor of the juice.

Oil is whisked in gradually once the acid base is created so that it will emulsify or suspend in the acid to give it a smoother texture. (To free-up a hand to whisk while you're pouring, make a rat tail—yes, the kind your brother used to whip you with!—with a damp kitchen towel and form it into a circular bed to perch the bowl on. This will keep the bowl from moving around and you can use both hands to pour the oil and whisk).

All vinaigrettes should sit for several minutes after they're prepared to maximize their flavors, and most refrigerate very well for several days in an airtight container.

PARSLEY, RUTABAGA, AND APPLE PUREE

A member of the mustard family, rutabaga is a cross between turnips and cabbage, and has characteristics similar to both of them. Loaded with nutrients and fiber and low in calories, rutabaga's slightly sulfuric flavor is tamed with the addition of sweet apple and fluffy Yukon gold potatoes in this show-stopping recipe. Flakes of pureed fresh parsley bring out rutabaga's distinct and winning flavor in this deceptively simple dish that takes just minutes to prep but will last a lifetime in your memories. This is a perennial favorite on my holiday table. By adding stock and perhaps a little bit of cream, the puree or any remaining leftovers are quickly transformed into a heart- and soul-warming soup.

3 medium rutabagas, peeled
    and cut into 2-inch cubes
    (about 4 cups)
1 Golden Delicious apple
    (or another sweet apple
    variety), cored and
    quartered with skin on
1 Yukon gold potato, peeled and
    cut into 2-inch cubes
1 cup water
Salt and freshly ground pepper
2 tablespoons sour cream
2 tablespoons butter
1/4 cup fresh parsley leaves, stiff
    stems removed

Combine the rutabaga, apple, potato, water, and an initial seasoning of salt and pepper in a medium-size pot. Bring to a boil over high heat and then reduce heat to a simmer. Cover and cook until the vegetables are fork tender, about 35 to 40 minutes.

Remove from the heat. Drain off all but 1/4 cup of the cooking liquid (reserve as a vegetable stock for later use in a soup or sauce) and add sour cream, butter, and parsley to the pot with the cooked produce and cooking liquid. Puree with a hand-held blender or process in the bowl of a food processor until very smooth. Taste and adjust seasoning. Serve immediately alongside pork or another roast with a generous dollop of creamery-fresh butter.

NOTE: The puree can be stored overnight in an airtight container in the refrigerator. Reheat over moderate heat before serving.

Serves 8

OVEN-ROASTED ASPARAGUS
WITH GRAPE TOMATOES IN WARM BACON VINAIGRETTE

Most of us associate the delicate, elegant spears of fresh asparagus with spring and fancy dinners, but due to some new farming techniques and the South's longer growing season, it can be enjoyed in the fall as well. The technique is called "forcing," and is done with potatoes, strawberries, and other double-crop varieties.

No matter what the season, asparagus is best if eaten within 24 hours of being cut. Until then, store upright in a bowl or glass with an inch or two of fresh water. As with so many vegetables, roasting magnifies the sweetness and tenderness of asparagus flavor, while lending smoky, earthy undertones. Serve the roasted asparagus in this recipe simply fresh from the oven, or garnish it with the warm grape-tomato salad for eye-popping color and mouth-popping panache.

2 bunches fresh asparagus,
    rinsed and tough ends
    removed
2 tablespoons olive oil
Salt and freshly ground pepper

FOR THE TOMATO SALAD

6 pieces bacon, diced
1 shallot, minced
¼ cup cider vinegar
⅓ cup extra virgin olive oil
2 teaspoons local honey
2 teaspoons Dijon mustard
Salt and freshly ground pepper
1 cup quartered (lengthwise)
    grape tomatoes

Preheat oven to 425 degrees. Toss the asparagus in the oil with some salt and pepper. Arrange in a single layer on a roasting pan. Roast on the center rack of the preheated oven until crisp-tender, about 10 to 14 minutes.

Meanwhile, sauté the bacon over medium-high heat until just crisp, about 5 minutes. Add the shallot, reduce heat to medium and sauté until translucent, about 3 minutes. Drain off all but 1 tablespoon of the rendered bacon fat. Whisk in vinegar, oil, honey, and mustard, stirring to scrape up any brown bits. Season to taste with salt and pepper. Toss together in a medium bowl with the tomatoes.

To serve, arrange the asparagus on a platter and top with the tomato salad.

Serves 6–8

FRESH SWEET ONION AND TOMATO GRATIN

Cool, late winter and early spring days feel warmer with this hearty, crunchy yet smooth gratin. The acidic nature of tomatoes plays nicely layered with the mild sweetness of the onions and the creaminess of the Brie. A long, slow bake in the oven sweetens the early, non-local tomatoes (unless they come from local hothouses) you'll likely find in the spring. This side dish would lovingly complete a roasted leg of lamb or a simple omelet.

FOR THE GRATIN

5 tablespoons butter, divided

3 medium fresh sweet onions, trimmed, quartered, and thinly sliced

Salt and freshly ground pepper

2 medium tomatoes, thinly sliced

FOR THE CUSTARD

1¼ cups whole milk

2 eggs

4 tablespoons chopped fresh parsley

2 tablespoons chopped fresh basil

¼ cup finely chopped sweet onion greens (from tops of the onions)

Salt and freshly ground pepper

FOR THE TOPPING

1 cup unseasoned breadcrumbs

Zest of 1 lemon

Salt and freshly ground pepper

6 (1-inch-long) slices Brie

Preheat oven to 350 degrees. Heat 3 tablespoons butter in a large sauté pan over medium heat. Add the onions, and then season with salt and pepper. Cook, stirring occasionally until softened, about 12 to 15 minutes; set aside to cool. Coat a deep-dish 9-inch pie pan or gratin dish with the remaining butter.

Meanwhile, prepare the custard. Combine all of the ingredients in a small bowl and whisk until smooth; set aside.

To prepare the topping, combine the breadcrumbs with the zest and seasonings in a small bowl.

To assemble, drain any excess liquid off the cooked onions. Distribute about one-third of the onions evenly on the bottom of the buttered pan. Top with a single layer of sliced tomatoes. Top with half of the remaining onions, another layer of tomato, and finish with remaining onions. If needed, season lightly with salt and pepper. Pour the custard mix over the entire surface of the layered onions and tomatoes. Top with cheese, spaced about 3 to 4 inches apart, along the top of the gratin. Finish with an even layer of the breadcrumb mixture.

Bake until golden and bubbly and the custard has set, about 35 to 40 minutes. If desired, finish under a hot broiler or a flame torch for an extra golden glow. Allow to sit for 10 to 15 minutes before slicing into wedges or squares.

NOTE: The gratin can be prepared ahead, covered and refrigerated, and then baked just before serving.

Serves 6–8

SPINACH AND MESCLUN SALAD
WITH FRESH STRAWBERRIES AND SWEET-HOT PECANS

The earliest yields of Southern spring harvests include sweet, plump, ripe strawberries and tender leaves of spinach, mesclun, and baby lettuces. Paired with sugar and paprika-coated pecans pulled hot from the sauté pan, a port vinaigrette, and the clean bite of mint, these spring produce belles are as beautiful, yet demure, as can be. If you come across a mellow, soft local cheese, it would be lovely scattered across the top before serving.

14 large strawberries, stemmed and halved (vertically)

⅓ cup balsamic vinegar

FOR THE VINAIGRETTE

1 shallot, minced

1 tablespoon Dijon mustard

1 tablespoon local honey

1 tablespoon red wine vinegar

Salt and freshly ground pepper

½ cup extra virgin olive oil

FOR THE PECANS

2 tablespoons extra virgin olive oil

½ cup pecan halves

1 tablespoon sugar

Dash of paprika

Salt and freshly ground pepper

FOR THE SALAD

2 cups fresh spinach

4 cups mesclun

8 leaves fresh mint

Goat cheese

Up to 1 hour before serving, combine the strawberries in a small bowl with the balsamic vinegar. Toss and marinate for at least 30 minutes, but no more than 1 hour. Strain the berries, reserving the juices; place berries in the refrigerator until ready to use.

To prepare the vinaigrette, combine the strained juices from the berries with the shallot, mustard, honey, vinegar, and salt and pepper to taste in a small bowl. Gradually incorporate the oil, whisking well to emulsify. Taste and verify seasonings.

In the meantime, heat 2 tablespoons oil over medium-high heat in a small sauté pan. Add the pecans, sugar, paprika, salt, and pepper. Toss and watch, toasting until the nuts turn a light golden brown; drain on a paper towel.

To serve, toss the spinach, mesclun, mint, goat cheese, and a bit of salt and pepper together in a large bowl with a light dressing of the vinaigrette (you probably will only need about half—save the rest for later). Serve on individual plates or on a large platter garnished with the marinated strawberries and warm pecans.

Serves 6

SAUTÉ OF GREEN BEANS
AND ROASTED PEPPERS IN A CATALINA SAUCE WITH FRESH GOAT CHEESE AND ALMONDS

Seducing kids into eating their veggies isn't always a simple task. In this dish, the bright flavors of a good-quality Catalina dressing helps get the kid in all of us more excited about green beans. It's a variation on a recipe theme a friend of mine used to prepare for her children when they were younger and fussier.

Now that they're all grown up, veggies hold real, across-the-board appeal to their palates—more proof that early and broad exposure to healthy eating styles has a lasting and positive impact. Fresh goat cheese and crunchy almonds dress this up for a warm-weather dinner party. Use only the best-quality prepared Catalina (or substitute French) dressing, or make your own.

I red bell pepper
I green bell pepper
3 cups fresh green beans, snapped and rinsed
3 cloves garlic, minced
I tablespoon olive oil
1/3 cup coarsely chopped almonds
1/4 cup top-quality Catalina dressing
Salt and freshly ground pepper
4 ounces fresh goat cheese (preferably from a local farmers market)

Roast the whole peppers under a hot broiler, turning at quarter points, until they are charred black all over. Run the peppers under cold water and remove skins, seeds, and cores. Pat the peppers dry and cut into a julienne (see Julienne Know-How, page 37).

Bring a large pot of generously salted water to a boil over high heat. Blanche the beans until just tender, plunging all at once into rapidly boiling water and cooking for about 3 minutes. Drain, then rinse beans in very cold water until they're cool. Drain and set aside or store overnight in the refrigerator for later use.

When close to serving, sauté the garlic in the oil in a large sauté pan over medium-low heat until softened, about 3 minutes. Increase the heat to medium-high. Add the almonds, blanched green beans, dressing, salt, and pepper. Toss and heat through for about 2 minutes. Season and drizzle each serving with crumbled fresh goat cheese. Serve immediately.

NOTE: This could also be chilled and served later over fresh greens tossed in a bit more Catalina dressing.

Serves 6

RED CABBAGE SLAW
WITH BACON, SCALLIONS, TOASTED PECANS, AND ROQUEFORT

The brilliant color contrasts of purple and green and substantive additions of bacon and Roquefort (or any variation on blue cheese) make this a high-style natural for a holiday meal, but because of cabbage's long season, this can be prepared virtually any time of the year. In spring, substitute green tops of fresh sweet spring onions for the scallions.

I first came across this flavor pairing years ago when I was working at a restaurant in Minneapolis. Not surprisingly, in that frigid land, this salad variation was prepared warm. I prefer it at room temperature, however. Add the garnishes at the last moment and enjoy!

1 medium head red cabbage, cored, quartered, and thinly sliced
¼ cup balsamic vinegar
⅓ cup extra virgin olive oil
Salt and freshly ground pepper

GARNISHES

4 scallions, cleaned and finely diced
⅓ cup Roquefort cheese, crumbled (or substitute fresh, artisanal goat cheese)
7 slices bacon (preferably sustainable)
½ cup coarsely chopped pecans
½ teaspoon sugar

Trim the tough outer leaves off of the cabbage and discard. Cut the cabbage in half lengthwise and then cut out the core and discard. Cut the halves in half again, lengthwise. Slice each quarter into very thin, consistent ⅛-inch-thick slices. Toss to coat in a large bowl with vinegar, oil, salt, and pepper. Cover tightly with a damp kitchen towel and marinate at least 3 hours but no more than 5 hours at room temperature (or refrigerate to marinate overnight).

Rinse the scallions and trim off the root; dice finely and set aside. Crumble the Roquefort into chunky pieces and set aside. Cut the bacon into a ¼-inch dice and cook over medium-high heat until crispy and golden brown. Remove and place on paper towels to drain; set aside.

Discard all but ½ teaspoon of the reserved bacon fat. Heat in a medium skillet over medium heat. Add the pecans and cook until golden, tossing to prevent burning, about 3 minutes. Add the sugar, as well as salt and pepper to taste; set aside to drain on paper towels.

To serve, arrange a heaping stack of the marinated cabbage in the center of each plate. Sprinkle with the scallions and top with a light dusting of cheese, nuts, and bacon. Finish with a dash of freshly ground pepper and serve.

Serves 8

PECAN PICKING

Native to North America and harvested from Texas to Illinois, pecans are the Southern stuff of pecan pie and cool weather dreams. Pecans are drawn to long, warm growing seasons with temperate nighttime temperatures. Georgia is one of the largest commercial producers of pecans in the South.

You'll start seeing them at farmers markets about the time the air picks up the first autumnal chill and, happily, they'll hang around through the holidays. Pecans' high oil content means that they will oxidize and potentially turn rancid fairly quickly. Therefore, it's best to purchase pecans from a local grower and, better yet, to buy the nuts in their attractive tan and brown shell, where they're naturally protected. Store pecans in a cool, dry place out of direct sunlight. If you haven't managed to use them up by then, store pecans in the freezer in an airtight container. They should do well there from one to three years.

FIELD PEAS
À LA PROVENÇAL

The bright flavors of the French region of Provence—garlic, tomatoes, and olive oil—work surprisingly well with earthy field peas and thin streaks of fresh chard to create this warm and satisfying salad.

2 cups fresh field peas

2 tablespoons extra virgin olive oil

2 cloves garlic, minced

2 fresh tomatoes, peeled and coarsely chopped

Salt and freshly ground pepper

¼ teaspoon local honey

6 chard leaves, cleaned with stems removed and coarsely chopped

Freshly grated aged cheese (optional)

Simmer the peas in a pot of generously salted water until tender, up to 1 hour; drain well and set aside. Heat the oil over medium-high heat in a large sauté pan. Add the garlic and reduce heat to medium-low. Cook until translucent, about 5 minutes, stirring frequently. Add the tomatoes, salt, pepper, and honey. Cook together gently over medium heat until the tomatoes cook down into a coarse sauce, about 10 minutes.

Add the pre-cooked peas and fresh chard. Cook until the chard has just wilted, about 5 minutes over medium heat. Serve immediately. If desired, top with freshly grated aged cheese.

Serves 4

SPICY BEEF IN CRISP CUCUMBER BOATS

Years ago, a farmer told me a lot of her customers like to carve out the center seeds of summer cukes to form cool, edible boats for myriad fillings. Here, I use ground grass-fed beef. Feel free to mix it up with some of the hormone-free, sustainable ground pork or chicken you come across at your favorite farmers market.

4 medium cucumbers

2 tablespoons olive oil

1½ pounds ground grass-fed chuck

Salt and freshly ground pepper

½ red onion, peeled and finely chopped

2 cloves garlic, minced

10 fresh mint leaves, chopped

3 tablespoons chopped fresh cilantro

Pinch of red pepper flakes

Generous dash of hot sauce

Dash of Worcestershire sauce (optional)

Juice of ½ lime

1 teaspoon local honey

Peel the cucumbers and trim off the rounded ends to flatten them. Cut the cucumbers in half horizontally and gently scoop out and discard the seeds. If the bottom of the "boats" are wobbly, trim the bottom-side lightly so they sit flat and sturdy. Arrange in a single layer on a plate, seal with plastic wrap and refrigerate until ready to use. **NOTE:** Use within 3 to 5 hours for the crucial maximum crunch a cucumber should provide.

In a large sauté pan, heat the oil over medium-high heat. Add the beef, breaking up with a wooden spoon as it browns. Season with salt and pepper. Cook until the meat is cooked through and lightly browned, about 10 minutes. Remove from the pan and drain well in a colander to remove most of the excess fat.

When cooled to room temperature, toss with the remaining ingredients in a medium-size bowl. Taste and adjust seasonings as needed. Cover tightly and refrigerate up to 5 hours to help develop more intense flavors. Before serving, bring to room temperature, which also intensifies the flavor. Taste and adjust seasoning once again. Fill each cucumber boat with about ¼ cup meat salad, shaping gently with a spoon or your hands to create attractive salad mounds.

Serve as a first course salad, or even as a main course on a hot summer evening when cooking and eating a heavy meal is simply not an option! Dress each plate with fresh cilantro and several thin slices of fresh lime. Serve while the cukes are cool.

Serves 4

YELLOW AND RED
WATERMELON SALSA OVER RED LEAF LETTUCE AND SMOKED HAM SALAD

Like tomatoes, watermelons are increasingly showing up at Southern farmers markets in a range of colors and sizes. This recipe puts both the sunny-hued "Yellow Flesh" and bright red "Cannonball" watermelon varieties to good use in a zippy, cool salsa served over a simply dressed salad of summer-seasonal red leaf lettuce and cubes of sautéed smoked ham. Mix and match with whatever local and seasonal watermelon you find. Freshness is always the key, and local is always how to find it.

FOR THE SALSA

1 cup each cubed "Yellow Flesh" and "Cannonball" watermelon (or another variety), seeded and cut into 1/4-inch cubes

10 mint leaves, cut into thin strips

3 tablespoons finely diced red onion

Dash of lime juice

Salt and freshly ground pepper

FOR THE SALAD

1 head red leaf lettuce, cleaned and gently dried

1 tablespoon olive oil

1 tablespoon butter

1 1/2 cups diced smoked ham

Salt and freshly ground pepper

FOR THE VINAIGRETTE

Juice of 1 lime

2 tablespoons fresh orange juice

1 tablespoon local honey

Salt and freshly ground pepper

1/4 cup extra virgin olive oil

To prepare the salsa, combine all salsa ingredients in a small bowl and chill up to 30 minutes before serving.

To prepare the salad, clean and dry the lettuce and tear into bite-size pieces. Reserve in a bowl, covered with a damp kitchen cloth, in the refrigerator.

Meanwhile, heat the oil and butter over medium-high heat in a large sauté pan. Cook ham, tossing occasionally, until golden brown on the edges. Season with salt and pepper. Set aside, keeping warm.

To prepare the vinaigrette, whisk together the juices, honey, salt, and pepper in a small bowl. Gradually drizzle in the oil, whisking the entire time to incorporate. Taste and verify seasoning; set aside.

To assemble, season the lettuce and dress it lightly with the vinaigrette; toss gently to coat. Arrange the greens on serving plates and top with a generous portion of the chilled salsa. Sprinkle warm ham over the top and the edges of each plate. Serve immediately.

Serves 4–6

SUMMER'S WATERMELON WINDFALL

Areas of the Southeast that have hot and humid growing conditions and slightly acidic, sandy loam soil are the most conducive to growing high-quality watermelons. They come in many types with an ever-increasing variety of quirky, appetite-inducing names, from All Sweet to Ice Box to Seedless. Within the types, there are a host of varieties (like the Yellow Flesh and Cannonball watermelons in this recipe) that come in different sizes, weight, flesh color, and shape.

Though not a widely known fact, all parts of the watermelon, including the seeds and the rind, are edible. Look for watermelons that are firm, heavy for their size, and bruise-free, with a creamy yellow underside and blossom end. Wash and dry your hands and watermelon before slicing it. Any leftover cut watermelon should be tightly covered and will store for up to one week in the refrigerator.

SWEET AND CREAMY SUMMER SQUASH CASSEROLE

Summer squash casseroles permeate the South like so many beads of August sweat. They're a staple at Sunday supper, alongside a plate of fried chicken and stewed butter beans. In this light version of what's commonly a savory custard-based dish, yellow squash's delicate flavor is amplified by removing excess water with salt. Wine, cream, herbs, and cheese bring it to a fine finish. Select, treat, and store summer squash as you would zucchini (See "Zucchini Picking," page 21).

5 yellow summer squash,
    scrubbed and tips removed
1 tablespoon salt
1 tablespoon olive oil
1 small onion, chopped
2 cloves garlic, minced
Salt and freshly ground pepper
1 tablespoon white wine
1/2 cup heavy cream
1/4 cup chopped fresh chives
1/4 cup grated Swiss cheese
1/4 cup grated Parmesan cheese

Grate the squash with a medium-size grater over a large bowl. Toss with 1 tablespoon salt and allow to sit for 10 minutes. Squeeze out excess water in batches by forming balls between your hands and squeezing. Discard excess fluid and set aside drained squash.

Heat the oil in a large sauté pan over medium heat. Add the onion and garlic and sauté until translucent, about 5 minutes. Add the squash and continue to sauté until just tender and most of the juices have reduced, another 5 minutes or so. Season with salt and pepper. Add the wine and increase heat to medium-high. Cook for 2 minutes, or until the wine has reduced to almost nothing, stirring constantly. Add the cream and reduce the heat to medium. Cook another 5 minutes, or until liquid is reduced by three-quarters. Stir in the chives.

Preheat broiler to high. Pour the squash mixture into a 4-quart gratin or baking dish. Allow to cool slightly and then sprinkle with the cheeses. Cook in the middle of the oven until heated through and bubbling on top, about 20 minutes; serve warm. This works as a great side dish for roasted chicken or pork, or as a meal with a green salad.

Serves 6–8

SAUTÉED EGGPLANT TRIFECTA

The mild sweetness of alternative thin-skinned and non-bitter eggplant varieties (like white, neon, and zebra) you'll find at farmers markets beg for consummate simplicity in cooking. Though traditionally paired with tomatoes and zucchini (think ratatouille), a flash sauté with a little bit of olive oil, fresh herbs, and garlic make these eggplant babies virtually wail in way-to-go bare bones cooking glee. Buy the absolute freshest eggplant you can find (which means firm, unpuckered and unblemished skin) and use it within 2 days of purchase. Use a hot pan and hot good-quality olive oil to reduce the amount of oil even the freshest eggplant will literally "sponge" up.

3 tablespoons olive oil

1 medium white eggplant,
    chopped in 1/4-inch cubes

1 medium neon eggplant,
    chopped in 1/4-inch cubes

1 medium zebra eggplant,
    chopped in 1/4-inch cubes

Salt and freshly ground pepper

2 cloves garlic, minced

2 tablespoons freshly
    chopped basil

Heat the oil over medium-high heat in a large sauté pan. When sizzling hot, add the eggplant, toss, and season with salt and pepper. Continue cooking for 1 minute. Add the garlic and reduce heat to medium. Cook through until soft, about 4 to 5 minutes. Taste and adjust seasonings. Add basil and toss just before serving. Serve immediately.

Serves 4

HORSERADISH CHEESE GRITS
WITH CONFETTI OF ROASTED POBLANO PEPPERS AND RED ONIONS

In the South, grits are served every way from here to Sunday and are as sacred as good manners and sweet tea. The mildness and gritty, nurturing texture render them an idyllic backdrop for shrimp, tomatoes, sausage—you name it!

I love the way the pungency of horseradish plays along with the grits, the smoky heat of roasted poblano peppers, and the sweetness of red onions in this versatile and easy-to-prepare side dish. Roasting is a great way to cut back a bit on any pepper's pungency while stepping up its sweetness. Serve this as a bed for the "Happy Pigs" Hot Pepper Jelly Glazed–Pork Chops (page 120) and a side of Oven-Roasted Asparagus (page 71) or grilled onions (page 62) for a plucky, porcine feast.

3 cups whole milk

¾ teaspoon salt

¼ teaspoon ground pepper

¾ cup stone-ground grits (yellow, white, or a blend)

2 poblano peppers

1 tablespoon olive oil

½ large red onion, thinly sliced

Salt and freshly ground pepper

¾ cup grated aged white cheddar cheese

2 tablespoons prepared horseradish

Bring milk, salt, and pepper to a boil in a medium saucepan. Pour in grits and whisk vigorously to blend. Reduce heat to medium-low and continue cooking, stirring every 1 to 2 minutes until thickened, about 40 to 45 minutes, adding more liquid (water or milk) as needed.

Meanwhile, heat the broiler (or flame grill) to high. Place the peppers directly under the hot broiler (or on the hot flames) and cook, turning occasionally, until blistered and blackened on all surfaces, about 3 to 5 minutes for each exposed surface; set aside to cool. Once cooled, run the peppers under a stream of cool water and pull off the blackened skin, seeds, and stem and discard. Stack the roasted pepper flesh and cut into thin, ¼-inch-wide, 2-inch-long strips; set aside.

In a medium skillet, heat the oil over medium-low heat. Add the onion, salt, and pepper, and cook, stirring occasionally, until softened and lightly browned, about 20 minutes.

To finish, stir the cheese into the cooked grits until melted. Gently fold in the horseradish, roasted pepper, and sautéed onions. Taste and adjust seasonings if necessary. Serve immediately or keep warm for up to 3 hours over a gently simmering water bath.

Serves 6

BRAISED FIGS AND SHALLOTS
IN A HONEY–RED WINE SAUCE

Of all fruits, figs somehow seem to me the most heaven-sent. Maybe it has to do with the whole Garden of Eden thing. Maybe it's their regal purple hue. It's certainly their sensual plumpness; the way they gently burst with sweetness and are gone in three tempting, juicy bites. Versatile and nutritious, their seasonal window is sadly a short-lived one, and they are highly perishable.

Use them the day you find them, or if you have to, store them in the refrigerator for no more than one or two days before you consume them. Lightly puree any leftovers in your food processor and serve it over room-temperature goat cheese with crackers for an instant appetizer.

2 tablespoons butter

30 large shallots, peeled

1 tablespoon finely chopped fresh sage

6 fresh figs, stems removed and cut into quarters, lengthwise

2 tablespoons local honey

Full-flavored red wine (such as a Cabernet Sauvignon) to cover by half

1 cup good-quality beef stock demi-glace (can be purchased at specialty food stores, or substitute beef stock)

Salt and freshly ground pepper

Melt the butter in a large, deep skillet over medium-high heat. Add the shallots and sage. Sauté about 4 minutes, tossing occasionally, until the shallots become slightly golden. Add the remaining ingredients. Reduce heat to low and cover. Simmer about 30 to 45 minutes, or until the shallots are fork-tender and the figs have broken down into a chunky compote.

Remove the cover and increase the heat to high. Cook until the liquid is reduced to a glaze that coats the shallots. Taste and adjust seasonings. Serve immediately with a light sprinkle of fresh chopped sage or garnish with whole, fresh leaves.

Serves 6–8

TWICE-BAKED SWEET POTATOES

This delicious recipe was generously provided by Sheri Castle, a cooking columnist, cooking instructor, and food writer who regularly distributes her recipes at the Carrboro Farmers' Market in Carrboro, North Carolina. This recipe puts the South's celebrated sweet potato to wholesome, satisfying, and original good use. Note that in this recipe, rather than being loaded with the added fat and calories of excessive cream and butter (like traditional twice-baked potatoes), much of the flavor and nutrition come from collards.

4 medium sweet potatoes
   (of equal size)
1/2 cup butter
1/3 cup cream
4 slices bacon, chopped
1 sweet onion, chopped
2 cloves garlic, minced
3 cups stemmed and shredded
   collard greens or other
   sturdy greens
2/3 cup chicken stock
2 teaspoons fresh thyme
1/2 cup grated Parmesan cheese
Salt and freshly ground pepper
1/2 cup grated Gruyère cheese

Preheat the oven to 350 degrees. Pierce the potatoes in several places with a fork. Place them in a single layer in the oven (it's a good idea to put a sheet of foil on the rack below them to catch any drips) and roast until tender, about 1 hour. Remove from the oven. When cool enough to handle, cut each potato in half lengthwise and use a spoon to scoop out the flesh, leaving a 1/4-inch-thick shell; set the shells aside. Place the flesh in a bowl and mash until smooth with a hand-held potato masher or run through a food mill. Stir the butter and cream into the warm puree and set aside.

Cook the bacon in a skillet over medium heat until crispy; drain on paper towels and set aside. Pour off all but 1 tablespoon of the drippings and add the onion to the skillet, stirring often, until completely soft, about 8 minutes. Add the garlic, collards, and stock. Cover the pan and cook, stirring occasionally, until the collards are tender, about 20 minutes. Uncover and cook until any remaining liquid evaporates. Stir the collards, thyme, and Parmesan cheese into the potato puree. Season with salt and pepper and stir in the reserved bacon. Divide the puree mixture evenly among the 8 potato shells. Place on a baking sheet and top each with Gruyère cheese. Bake until the cheese is melted and the potatoes are heated through, about 30 minutes. Serve warm.

Serves 8

LOCAL HONEY–DRIZZLED CHEESE TOASTS

The combination of fragrant local honey, crunchy, good bread, and a pungent, fresh cheese is absolutely ambrosial. Incredibly, I first put the combo together all those years ago when living in the tiny village of Chalabre, France, where fresh, oven-warm bread, local honey, and an array of cheeses were within a two-minute walk from my front doorstep. These little toasts were my breakfast on most mornings.

Artisanal cheeses (especially goat cheese), local honey, and good, crusty bread are de rigeur at farmers markets throughout the market season. This combo is beyond heavenly. These toasts are great for a heartwarming breakfast, as an hors d'oeuvre, or as a side to an omelet or salad any time of year.

1 loaf French baguette bread or a more rustic country or whole grain bread

1½ pounds pungent soft cheese, such as fresh goat cheese, Camembert, or Brie

About ½ cup local honey

Preheat broiler to high. Slice the bread in half horizontally and cut into 4- to 6-inch lengths. Top each with a generous slice or portion of cheese. Broil in the center of the oven until the edges of the bread have browned and the cheese is bubbling, about 5 minutes. Watch carefully so the cheese doesn't burn. Remove from the oven and place a couple of toasts on individual serving plates. Drizzle each serving with a tablespoon or two of honey. Serve immediately.

Makes 8–10 toasts

HONEY, HERE'S TO YOUR HEALTH!

Honey's been used for centuries as a topical application to ward off infection due to its natural potent antiseptic and antibacterial qualities. The practice was largely abandoned with the onset of antibiotics in the last century, but honey's been making a comeback in pharmaceutical circles as an important player in mass-marketed topical ointments designed to promote healing and reduce infection.

Consuming local, raw honey from the area where you live has been shown to reduce sensitivity to hay fever and other allergens. Locally harvested honey is readily found at farmers markets across the Southeast, each bearing the signature flavors and aromas of the meadows and flowers in the worker bee's verdant, nectar-feeding domain.

HEART OF THE MATTER MAINS

EARLY SPRING AND FALL
Fresh Sweet Potato Ravioli with Sautéed Tat Soi, Roasted Garlic, and Honey-Toasted Walnuts in a Brown Butter Sauce 102

SPRING
Roasted Garlic-Flavored Fresh Spaghetti with English Peas, Pancetta, and Leeks in a Cream Sauce 105

Vidalia Onion Tart with Bacon, Local Honey, and Fresh Thyme 106

Sweet River Run Farms Grass-Fed Beef Meat Loaf 108

SUMMER THROUGH FALL
Wine-Poached Salmon with Cucumber Crudité Sauce 110

Tomato and Arugula Tart 111

Stuffed Eggplant Parmesan 113

Sautéed Flounder with Fresh Tomato, Corn, and Avocado Salsa 114

FALL
Soulful Braised Pork with Fresh Cider and Winesap Apples 116

FALL THROUGH WINTER
Curried Roasted Pumpkin with Lentils 117

Creamy Citrus Shrimp and Fettucine 118

YEAR-ROUND
"Happy Pigs" Hot Pepper Jelly–Glazed Pork Chops 120

FRESH SWEET POTATO RAVIOLI
WITH SAUTÉED TAT SOI, ROASTED GARLIC,
AND HONEY-TOASTED WALNUTS IN
A BROWN BUTTER SAUCE

While fresh pasta and cooking staples like artisanal cheeses, eggs, meats, and other non-vegetable options are increasingly making the rounds at Southern farmers markets, tat soi is in its nascent stage. I've just started coming across it on a regular basis, but when I do, I'm sure to add a bunch or two to my shopping cache.

A lovely, buttery, and mildly mustard-flavored Asian green, tat soi is reminiscent of an amalgam of kale and arugula. Fabulous raw or cooked, it adds deep green color and a cornucopia of nutrients and fiber to this hearty and satisfying dish, which is perfect on any chilly day. The inclusion of local honey and orange zest gives it festive, special occasion–worthy flair.

ADVANCE PREP

1 head garlic

2 tablespoons olive oil, divided

1 bunch fresh tat soi, well washed, patted dry, and cut into 2-inch squares (yields about 5 cups)

Salt and freshly ground pepper

FOR THE WALNUTS

1 tablespoon butter

1/2 cup coarsely chopped walnuts

Salt and freshly ground pepper

1 teaspoon wild honey

FOR THE PASTA

16 fresh sweet potato ravioli (or substitute black pepper linguine, cheese ravioli, or fresh pasta of choice)

3 tablespoons salt

Preheat oven to 425 degrees. Trim the papery top off the garlic head to expose the top of the cloves. Drizzle with 1 tablespoon oil and wrap the entire bulb with a small piece of aluminum foil. Bake until softened, about 25 minutes.

Meanwhile, heat a skillet over medium-high heat and add remaining oil. When just sizzling, add the tat soi, season with salt and pepper, and cook, stirring, until wilted, about 3 minutes; set aside.

In another medium skillet, prepare the walnuts. Melt the butter in the skillet over high heat. When bubbling and warm, add the walnuts, toss to coat, and season with salt and pepper. Reduce heat to medium-high and cook 2 to 3 minutes, or until the walnuts have begun to turn golden. Add honey and coat; drain the nuts on a paper towel and reserve.

Prepare the pasta according to package directions. Drain the pasta, reserving 2 tablespoons of the cooking water. **NOTE:** In general, fresh pasta takes much less time to cook than dry pasta. However, it still needs lightly boiled water, plenty of salt, and a tender touch—especially ravioli. Stir with care and be sure not to subject it to a hard boil, which could tear it apart. It's always

continued on page 104

¼ cup butter
Reserved roasted garlic cloves
Salt and freshly ground pepper
Zest of 1 orange

done when it floats! You can usually count on approximately 4 minutes of cooking time for fresh or frozen ravioli.

To prepare the sauce and assemble the dish, melt butter in a large, deep skillet over medium-high heat until a light, golden brown. Squeeze the roasted garlic cloves out of the roasted garlic head and into the pan; discard the papery skins, and then toss the cloves to coat and brown. Season with salt and pepper and add the zest. Pour the browned butter over the sautéed tat soi and add the reserved 2 tablespoons of the ravioli cooking water and the reserved ravioli. Sauté all together quickly over high heat and toss gently with the ravioli. Serve on a large platter or as individual portions topped with the honey-toasted walnuts.

Serves 4

TAT SOI TIPS

Though best served within a day or two of purchase, tat soi is a resilient beast and will easily last for up to one week in your refrigerator, wrapped in a lightly dampened kitchen towel. Don't wash tat soi until just before using, but when you do, wash it well. Tat soi's creviced, wavy leaves can hold soil. Trim the stalks and submerge the leaves in a sink or large bowl of cool water, swishing to release the dirt and grit. Drain off the water and repeat until the rinsing water is clear. It usually takes about 3 to 4 swishes.

ROASTED GARLIC-FLAVORED FRESH SPAGHETTI WITH ENGLISH PEAS, PANCETTA, AND LEEKS IN A CREAM SAUCE

The versatility of fresh pasta at Southern farmers markets is growing by leaps and bounds. This recipe employs earthy, roasted garlic fresh spaghetti. The toothsome texture of fresh pasta trumps that of dried, and the impact of the flavor and clinginess of the pasta readily embrace the cream-based sauce and sweetness of spring peas. Cook most fresh pasta within 2 to 3 days of purchase or freeze for several months for optimal texture and flavor freshness.

1 cup English or seasonal
  fresh peas (pods removed),
  blanched and refreshed

FOR THE CREAM SAUCE

1 tablespoon olive oil
2 (¼-inch-thick) slices pancetta
  or another aged artisanal
  ham, diced
1 leek, green stalk removed,
  cleaned and cut into a
  ¼-inch dice
3 tablespoons dry white wine
¼ cup chicken stock
¼ cup whole cream
Salt and freshly ground pepper
2 servings roasted garlic-
  flavored fresh spaghetti (or
  another compatible flavor,
  such as plain or peppered)
¼ cup freshly grated Parmesan
  or Pecorino cheese
Finely chopped fresh tarragon

Remove the peas from the pods and rinse well. Bring a few cups of salted water to a boil and add the peas. Blanch for 2 to 3 minutes, drain, and refresh under running cold water; set aside.

To prepare the sauce, heat the oil in a large sauté pan over medium-high heat. Add the pancetta and toss to coat. Cook until the pancetta is brown and most of the excess fat has been rendered. Drain off any excess fat and reduce the heat to medium. Add the leek and sauté over medium-low heat, stirring. Cook until just softened (but not browned), about 2 to 3 minutes. Add the wine and cook until it has reduced to almost nothing. Add the stock and cook until reduced by half. Add cream and heat through. Season with salt and pepper, keeping in mind that the pancetta and cheese are both salty (so going light on the salt is a good idea). Set aside for up to 1 hour.

Just before you're ready to serve, bring a large pot of salted water to a boil. Add the pasta and stir. Cook until just tender, about 2 to 3 minutes, and drain. While that's cooking, add the peas to the sauce and heat through over medium heat. Add the cooked pasta, peas, and cheese to the pan. Toss to distribute evenly. Serve immediately, garnished with a few sprigs of finely chopped fresh tarragon to garnish, if desired.

Serves 2

VIDALIA ONION TART
WITH BACON, LOCAL HONEY, AND FRESH THYME

The official vegetable of Georgia since 1990, the sweet, mild Vidalia onion is recognized worldwide for its gentle flavor. However, Vidalias can only be grown in a 20-county production area in and around Vidalia, Georgia, to legally wear the Vidalia label. Because of their thin, tender skins and relatively high sugar content, Vidalia onions are more perishable than most and need to be consumed within about one week of purchase. Look for Georgia-grown Vidalias at farmers markets around the Southeast in early spring through the summer.

Although a regular white sweet spring onion would make a fine substitute, Vidalia's signature sweetness is gorgeous with the saltiness of bacon and the mild, lemony bite of fresh thyme in this savory tart. Serve with a salad and you've got a meal to remember. If you want to bypass making tart pastry, go ahead and buy prepared pastry at the grocery.

FOR THE PASTRY

3 cups all-purpose flour

1 cup cold, unsweetened butter, cut into 1-inch cubes

1 teaspoon salt

4 to 6 tablespoons ice water

FOR THE FILLING

4 slices bacon

5 large Vidalia onions, peeled, halved, and thinly sliced

Salt and freshly ground pepper

2 tablespoons coarsely chopped fresh thyme leaves

1/4 cup dry white wine

3 tablespoons local honey

1 egg, beaten

2 tablespoons whole cream

EQUIPMENT: 1 (12-inch) tart pan or 2 (9-inch) tart pans

To prepare the pastry, pulse together the flour, butter, and salt in the bowl of a food processor fitted with a plastic blade until the butter is about the size of small peas—about ten pulses. Gradually, drizzle in the ice water while pulsing. The amount needed will depend on the moisture content of the flour. Add just enough water for the dough to form a loose ball. Turn the pastry out onto a lightly floured surface and quickly form the dough into a 1-inch-thick disk. Wrap with plastic wrap and refrigerate for 30 minutes (or up to three days) to rest. Preheat oven to 375 degrees about 20 minutes before you're planning to bake the tart.

Meanwhile, prepare the filling. Heat a large sauté pan over medium-high heat. Add the bacon in a single layer and cook, turning as needed, until the bacon is crispy and the fat has been rendered. Remove the bacon to drain on paper towels to cool, chopping coarsely once cool enough to handle. Reserve 2 tablespoons of the bacon fat (discarding the rest or using for another purpose) in the pan and reduce the heat to medium. Add the onions, salt, pepper, and thyme. Cook over medium heat until the onions have softened, stirring frequently, about 15 minutes. Do not let the onions brown!

Add the wine and increase the heat to medium-high. Cook until the wine has cooked down to a glaze, about 3 minutes. Reduce the heat to medium-low and add the honey and reserved chopped bacon. Stir and cook 5 minutes more. Remove the onion mixture from the heat and spoon into a shallow pan; refrigerate to cool. When cooled, drain off any excess pan juices and stir in the egg and cream. Adjust seasonings as needed.

To assemble, roll the reserved dough to ¼ inch thickness. Line the pan(s) with the pastry and form even edges. Refrigerate another 10 minutes, then line the pastry with parchment paper and fill with pie weights. Bake 20 to 25 minutes, or until lightly browned. Remove the paper and weights and bake another 15 to 20 minutes to brown the bottom. Allow to cool slightly before filling. Reduce the oven temperature to 350 degrees. Fill the pastry crust with the onion mixture and bake until golden brown and the filling is set, about 35 minutes.

Makes 10–12 servings

SWEET RIVER RUN FARMS GRASS-FED BEEF MEAT LOAF

Grass-fed beef tastes completely unlike the corn-fed, mass-produced, commercial variety found on grocery store shelves across the country. When cooking, the aromas of the sweet farm grasses upon which the cattle grazed during their gentle, low-stress, antibiotic- and hormone-free lives fills your home. It tastes exactly like it smells: clean, pure, grassy, and even a little nutty. The texture is firmer and more elastic than corn-fed beef, too. Because it has a lower fat content, grass-fed beef typically cooks more quickly. Be careful not to overcook it or it will become dry.

2 pounds (4 cups) grass-fed ground beef

1 cup whole wheat panko (or substitute other unseasoned fresh breadcrumbs)

1 cup skim milk

1 large egg

2 tablespoons Dijon mustard

1 tablespoon Worcestershire sauce

2 dashes Tabasco or preferred hot sauce brand

2 tablespoons ketchup

1 tablespoon soy sauce

1 tablespoon barbecue sauce

3 cloves garlic, smashed into a rough puree

¼ cup chopped fresh parsley

1 tablespoon freshly ground pepper

1½ teaspoons kosher or sea salt

4 tablespoons butter

Preheat oven to 325 degrees. Combine all of the ingredients except the butter in a large bowl and, using your hands, blend thoroughly. Press firmly into a 9-inch terrine mold or regular loaf pan, shaping to round the top slightly, like a traditional meat loaf. Cut the butter into several small squares and evenly dot the top of the meat loaf with the butter, pressing lightly with fingertips to embed. Bake on center rack until a knife inserted in the center comes out clean, about 25 minutes (or 45 minutes in a traditional loaf pan). Remove, and allow to rest about 15 minutes. Drain off any excess fat and turn out the loaf. Slice into 2-inch slices and then serve immediately. This is fabulous with the Fork-Smashed Red Potatoes and Scallions (page 77) and a heaping serving of Zesty Sautéed Lacinato Kale with Garlic (page 60).

Makes 8 servings

WHERE'S THE BEEF?

If it's grass-fed cattle, it's grazing lazily in an open field of waving, green grass, the way cows were meant to do.

Cows are healthier eating grass because that's what their stomachs are designed to process, not the corn and soybean diets fed to commercial cattle. Grass-fed beef is healthier for the consumer because it has a healthy ratio of Omega-6 and Omega-3 fatty acids, is lower in fat and calories than corn-fed beef, and has high levels of CLA, or conjugated linoleic acid, another good fat that's been shown to prevent cancer.

WINE-POACHED SALMON
WITH CUCUMBER CRUDITÉ SAUCE

The round, mellow flavors and soft, yielding texture of salmon poached in white wine provides the perfect flavor and texture counterpoint for a cool sauce of diced fresh cucumbers and spice. The fish can be served warm or at room temperature, which makes it extra flexible during the low-patience, high-heat days of Southern summers. I especially like the snowy white, slightly sweet essence of the Eureka cucumber variety in this dish, but use whatever's fresh and in season near you.

FOR THE SAUCE

1 medium Eureka cucumber (or suggested substitute), peeled, seeded, and finely diced

1 red bell pepper, seeded and finely diced

½ red onion, peeled and finely diced

1 jalapeño pepper, seeded and finely diced

2 cloves garlic, smashed

3 tablespoons white wine vinegar

2 tablespoons sugar

½ cup water

Salt and freshly ground pepper

FOR THE FISH

6 fresh salmon fillets (or substitute another mild, oily fish), deboned and skinned

2 cups good-quality white wine (Chardonnay, Muscadet, Pinot Grigio)

2 tablespoons salt

Basil, to garnish

To prepare the sauce, combine the cucumber, bell pepper, onion, jalapeño, and garlic in a medium bowl. Separately, combine the vinegar, sugar, and water in a smaller bowl. Stir to combine and dissolve the sugar. Pour this over the cucumber mixture and toss well to coat. Season with salt and pepper to taste. Cover and refrigerate at least 30 minutes and up to 3 hours (more and the cukes may become mushy). Bring back to room temperature before serving with the fish.

Prepare the fish once the sauce is at room temperature. Arrange the fillets in a single layer in a large, deep skillet. Cover halfway with the wine (you may need more or less depending on the size of the pan). Bring the wine to a simmer over medium-high heat. Add the salt. Cook until the fish is opaque nearly through to the center of the bottom side of the fillets, about 5 minutes. Gently flip each piece of fish with a spatula and repeat.

Remove the fish from the pan, draining off any excess fluid and patting with paper towels to remove excess water. Arrange the warm (or cool) fish on a plate and garnish each with several tablespoons of the sauce. Decorate with a large leaf of basil. Serve with steamed rice or Fork-Smashed Potatoes (page 77).

Serves 6

TOMATO AND ARUGULA TART

This gorgeous, savory tart gives a French twist to the beloved Southern tomato pie. Unlike the Southern version, I omit the mayonnaise altogether. Instead, I beef it up with a butter-rich, homemade pastry and plenty of fat, ripe tomatoes.

Either homemade or prepared pastry will work just fine. The keys here are plenty of luscious, fresh tomatoes and peppery arugula, which are both in season at the same time. Bring along an appetite for deliciousness before settling into this tomato-rich treat.

FOR THE PASTRY

3 cups all-purpose flour

Generous pinch of salt

¾ cup unsalted butter, chilled and chopped into large chunks

I egg yolk

Up to ½ cup ice water

FOR THE FILLING

4 tablespoons olive oil, divided

I medium shallot, finely chopped

8 cups clean, loosely packed arugula

Salt and freshly ground pepper

4 large ripe tomatoes, thinly sliced

I cup grated aged Parmigiano-Reggiano cheese

NOTE: Skip to the third paragraph if you're using a prepared pastry.

Preheat oven to 425 degrees. In the bowl of a food processor fitted with a plastic blade, pulse the flour, salt, and butter until the butter is the size of small peas—about 10 pulses. Add the egg yolk and pulse 2 to 5 times until incorporated. Gradually pour the ice water into the mixture while pulsing. Add only as much as it takes for the pastry to form a loose ball.

Place the pastry on a lightly floured surface and manipulate until it forms a ball. Flatten to a 2-inch-high disk and wrap tightly in plastic wrap. Refrigerate 20 to 30 minutes. **NOTE:** Extra dough can be frozen, similarly wrapped, for later use.

Roll out the chilled dough on a lightly floured surface to ¼ inch thickness. Line a tart pan with the pastry, shaping it gently into the pan with fingertips. Cut off excess edge, leaving about ¼ inch to form the border. Press the dough gently between your thumb and forefinger as you move along the circumference of the pan to "lift" and "shape" the dough into an even, smooth border. Refrigerate 10 minutes. Line the tart shell with aluminum foil and fill with pie weights or dried beans. Place the tart in the center of the oven and bake for 20 minutes. Reduce the heat to 350 degrees. Remove foil and pie weights, and continue to bake at reduced heat 15 minutes more; remove from oven and set aside.

continued on page 112

To prepare the filling, heat 3 tablespoons oil in a large sauté pan over medium-high heat. Add the shallot, reduce the heat to medium, and cook until translucent, about 5 minutes. Increase the heat to medium-high, add the arugula, season lightly with salt and pepper, and cook until the arugula has wilted, about 5 minutes; set aside to cool. Squeeze out any excess water in the arugula.

To fill the tart, line the pre-baked bottom with a thin, even layer of sautéed arugula. Top with the tomatoes, working in a circular pattern from the outer edge inward. Layer the tomatoes tightly upon each other, covering about half of each slice with the next slice. Drizzle with remaining oil and season lightly with salt and pepper. Sprinkle the grated cheese evenly over the top. Return to a 350-degree oven and bake until golden brown and bubbly, about 35 to 40 minutes. Finish under a hot broiler for a darker crust. Serve warm or at room temperature.

Serves 8

STUFFED EGGPLANT PARMESAN

*Either a firm, fresh Guinea eggplant or any of the shapely, multi-hued and more petite
Japanese varietals will work for this whimsical, pasta-free play on traditional eggplant
Parmesan. Just remember to alter the cooking times accordingly for more petite eggplant.
You'll know it's done when the eggplant gently yields to the weight of its cheesy, rich filling
and the top is bubbling and golden brown.*

1 medium Guinea eggplant or
   4 Japanese varietals
2 cups fresh tomato sauce, such
   as Endless Summer Tomato
   Sauce (see page 90)
3 tablespoons chopped fresh
   parsley
1 tablespoon chopped or
   coarsely torn fresh basil
½ cup crushed crackers or
   breadcrumbs
¾ cup ricotta cheese
Salt and freshly ground pepper
About ½ pound or 6 to 8
   slices fresh mozzarella

Preheat oven to 350 degrees. Cut the eggplant in half lengthwise.
Trim the rounded edges with a knife so that the halves will lay flat
on a roasting pan, cut-side up. Using a sharp-edged spoon, scoop
out the flesh, coarsely chop, and put in a medium bowl. Leave a
½-inch border around the interior of the eggplant; set aside.

Toss the chopped flesh with all the remaining ingredients except
the mozzarella. Taste the mixture to verify seasoning. Place the
eggplant halves on a baking or roasting pan, cut-side up. Fill each
halfway with the stuffing. Arrange 2 to 3 slices of mozzarella on
top. Finish with a layer of stuffing, shaping gently to round the
tops. Bake for 45 minutes to an hour, or until tender, bubbling,
and golden.

Serves 4–6

SAUTÉED FLOUNDER
WITH FRESH TOMATO, CORN, AND AVOCADO SALSA

Most fortuitously, the twin beauties of summer—corn and tomatoes—are in peak season at the same time of year. They work beautifully here, bound with the mellow, round flavor of (non-local, sorry) avocado and the milkiness of fresh, sautéed flounder. Though often fried, this fish is superb fresh from a hot pan cooked simply with a bit of olive oil and butter. The salsa can be made ahead since it gains flavor depth over time (up to 6 hours) and the fish is cooked in a flash, making this a cool dish for warm weather dining.

FOR THE SALSA

4 medium tomatoes, peeled, seeded, and diced
1/2 ripe avocado, peeled and diced
Juice of 1/2 lime
3 green onions, vertically sliced and chopped
Corn kernels cut from 1 ear of fresh, cooked corn
4 tablespoons chopped fresh basil
3 tablespoons chopped fresh chives
1/4 cup good-quality olive oil
2 cloves garlic, minced
4 saffron threads
Dash of local honey
Dash of cumin
Salt and freshly ground pepper

FOR THE FISH

6 flounder fillets (about 6 ounces each), skinned
1 tablespoon butter
1 tablespoon olive oil
Salt and freshly ground pepper
Fresh basil, chopped

To prepare the salsa, make the tomatoes easy to peel by submerging them in a pot of boiling water for 30 seconds, then removing and submerging in cold water. This will help the skin peel off; all you need to do is pull it off with your fingers or with the assistance of a paring knife. Gently combine the tomatoes and the remaining salsa ingredients in a medium bowl, folding with a wooden spoon to prevent breaking the avocados; season carefully to taste. Refrigerate and store for up to 6 hours. Bring to room temperature before serving.

Prepare the fish just minutes before serving. Rinse the fillets carefully and examine for any bones that need removal. Pat dry with a kitchen or paper towel. Heat a large nonstick skillet over medium-high heat. Add the butter and oil. Season the fish on both sides with salt and pepper. Place the fish in a single layer in the pan. Cook about 2 minutes on each side, flipping only once. When the fish is golden brown and just opaque in the center, serve immediately with a generous serving of room temperature salsa and a sprinkling of basil.

Serves 6

SOULFUL BRAISED PORK
WITH FRESH CIDER AND WINESAP APPLES

Comparing commercially grown apples to those grown and harvested at smaller, sustainable orchards is like comparing apples to, well, oranges. That's because commercial apple growers are frequently forced to pick the apples before they're fully ripe, unlike the smaller orchards (which supply farmers markets), where apples are picked ripe and fresh from the tree. The taste is incomparable. Of the many varieties that make it to market in the fall, the Winesap apple, with its crisp and juicy flesh and high crunch factor, is my frequent apple of choice for eating, cooking, and baking.

In this slowly braised medley of pork and apples, the fruit breaks down into a chunky, sweet gravy spiked with the acidic bite of fresh cider (do not use cider from concentrate!), sage, and rosemary. Pork butt, from the working muscles of a pig's shoulder, cooks down to fork-tender perfection with a long, slow braise that can go on for hours. The scents wafting seductively from the kitchen build an irresistible appetite for a feast.

1 tablespoon olive oil

1 tablespoon unsalted butter

2 pounds Boston Butt pork shoulder, cut into 2-inch cubes

1 teaspoon dried sage leaves

Salt and freshly ground pepper

1 medium onion, peeled, halved, and thinly sliced

2 stalks celery, thinly sliced

3 cloves garlic, minced

2 tablespoons all-purpose flour

2 cups fresh apple cider

1 cup water or chicken stock

2 Winesap apples, peeled, cored, and cut into 1/2-inch chunks

3 sprigs fresh rosemary, bound with a string

In a large Dutch oven or crockpot, heat the oil and butter over high heat until bubbling. Add the pork and sage, and season generously with salt and pepper. Brown the pork well on all sides, stirring occasionally, until the meat is colored a deep, golden brown. Remove the meat from the pan and set aside; reduce the heat to medium. Add the onion, celery, and garlic and cook until just softened and translucent, about 5 minutes, stirring occasionally.

Return the browned pork to the pan and dust with the flour. Stir to coat and cook through, about 3 minutes. Add the cider to deglaze the pan. Stir to release all of the browned bits from the pan. Add enough stock or water to cover by a little over half. Add the apples and rosemary and bring to a boil; reduce to a very low simmer over low heat. Cover loosely with a lid and cook until very tender and thickened, about 3 to 4 hours. Remove the rosemary bunch and taste to verify seasonings before serving.

(This recipe originally ran in the January/February 2008 issue of Lowcountry Living *magazine).*

Serves 6

CURRIED ROASTED PUMPKIN
WITH LENTILS

Cubes of pie pumpkin (also known as Sugar pumpkin) bake together with ginger, curry, cumin, lentils, and stock in this meatless hungry-man dish, infusing the house with festive scents of the season. Crunchy toasted pumpkin seeds give added crunch to this recipe, which is loaded with flavor, fiber, color, and nutrients.

3 tablespoons olive oil

1 large onion, minced

4 cloves garlic, sliced

1 cup uncooked dark lentils

1/4 teaspoon ground ginger

2 teaspoons curry

1 teaspoon cumin

Salt and freshly ground pepper

2 cups low-sodium chicken
stock (or substitute
vegetarian stock)

3 cups raw pumpkin, peeled
and cut into 1/4-inch cubes,
plus reserved seeds

1/3 cup currants

1/4 cup chopped fresh parsley,
plus more for garnish

1 teaspoon local honey

1/2 to 1 cup water, as needed

Fresh parsley, to garnish

FOR THE TOASTED PUMPKIN SEEDS

2 tablespoons butter

1 cup reserved pumpkin seeds,
rinsed and dried

Salt and freshly ground pepper

Preheat the oven to 375 degrees. Heat the oil in a large roasting pan over medium-high heat. Add the onion and garlic. Reduce heat to medium and sauté until softened, about 3 minutes.

Rinse the lentils and then add to pan and sauté for 1 minute. Add the ginger, curry, cumin, salt, pepper, and stock. Cover the pan tightly with aluminum foil and roast 10 minutes on the center rack of the oven. Remove the cover and add the pumpkin, currants, parsley, and honey. Depending on their moisture content, the lentils may have absorbed all or most of the stock. If so, add 1/2 cup to 1 cup water to the pan. Cover and continue to cook in the oven another 30 minutes, or until the lentils are crunchy-tender and the pumpkin is soft.

To prepare the pumpkin seeds, melt the butter over medium-high heat in a large skillet. Add seeds and season with salt and pepper. Cook, tossing frequently, until golden-colored and emitting a nutty aroma. Remove from the pan and drain on paper towels.

To serve, arrange the roasted pumpkin and lentil medley on a large serving platter or individual plates and garnish with a sprinkle of fresh parsley and the warm, toasted pumpkin seeds.

Serves 6

PUMPKIN-CUTTING PRECAUTIONS

Because of their dense rinds, pumpkins, like all winter squash, are difficult to peel when raw. Do so with caution! It helps to cut the pumpkin in half horizontally, seed it, then cut the pumpkin into long vertical wedges, like you would a melon. From there, pare the rind with a sharp knife and cut into the desired shape.

CREAMY CITRUS SHRIMP AND FETTUCCINE

The sweetness of shrimp (especially the local white shrimp available in Southern coastal areas in the cooler fall and winter months) just begs for an acidic edge, and it gets it here in threes—lemon, lime, and freshly squeezed orange juice. A dash of cream and a pat of butter smoothes out the edges like a creamy citrus cloud wrapped around broad, flat fettuccine noodles. Fast and easy, it makes for an ideal casual dinner party feast or a simple, fabulous meal anytime you can get your hands on fresh, local shrimp.

¾ pound fettucine, fresh
    or dried

1 tablespoon olive oil

1 tablespoon butter

¾ pound fresh, local shrimp,
    peeled with tails left on

Salt and freshly ground pepper

3 small cloves garlic, smashed
    and chopped

1 small shallot, finely chopped

Juice of ½ lemon

Juice of ½ lime

4 tablespoons freshly squeezed
    orange juice (do not
    substitute concentrate or
    you will pay for it in flavor!)

3 tablespoons clam juice

2 tablespoons capers

2 tablespoons chopped fresh
    thyme

¼ cup whole cream

1 tablespoon butter

Fresh thyme sprigs (optional)

For the pasta, bring a large pot of generously salted water to a boil. Cook the pasta according to package directions to al dente, or slightly firm to the bite. Start the shrimp sauté about 5 minutes before the pasta will be done so that the sauce and pasta will be done at the same time. This one comes together quickly!

For the sauté, combine the oil and butter in a large sauté pan heated over medium-high heat. Add the shrimp, season with salt and pepper, and sauté briefly, about 1 minute on each side, turning once to brown evenly. Reduce the heat to medium. Add the garlic and shallot; cook gently for about 1 minute. Add all of the juices. Cook until the liquid is reduced by half. Whisk in the remaining ingredients except the thyme sprigs and heat through over low heat; season to taste.

To finish, drain the pasta thoroughly. Add to the sauté pan and toss well. Serve immediately in individual bowls or on a platter. Garnish with fresh sprigs of thyme if desired.

(This modified recipe was originally published in the September/ October, 2006 issue of Lowcountry Living *magazine).*

Serves 4

SHRIMP STORAGE

Fresh shrimp refrigerates and freezes well. To store shrimp in the refrigerator, toss them with ice and place in a colander over some kind of a drainage receptacle, such as a deep bowl. It is very important to keep the ice fresh, replacing it and draining accumulated water so that the shrimp are not "sitting" in cold water, but rather, atop the ice. Stored like this, the shrimp will stay fresh for several days.

To freeze, first toss the shrimp in ice water. This will create a kind of protective coating to prevent freezer burn. Rather than using ubiquitous and not terribly eco-friendly plastic bags, try freezing the shrimp in an empty paper milk carton with some of the ice water, folding down the top to seal. Another bonus in using the carton is that the pesky shrimp tails cannot pierce a milk carton, which means you won't lose any of the protective ice water bath. Shrimp will freeze well for several months when properly stored.

"HAPPY PIGS" HOT PEPPER JELLY—GLAZED PORK CHOPS

Caw Caw Creek's gargantuan (average 10 to 16 ounces each) pork chops are spot-on great when glazed with the peppery heat of the hot pepper jellies available at most farmers markets throughout the season. Many jellies are prepared with the bounty of summer and fall's hot peppers. This type of jelly is frequently served over a wedge of cream cheese for an easy and impressive appetizer served up on crackers, which is good, indeed. But, on grilled heirloom pig, hot pepper jelly takes on whole hog, heavenly proportions!

Emile DeFelice of Caw Caw Creek Farms advises on his website (www.cawcawcreek. com) that the molecular structure of pork is different than beef, and "it does not want to be heated up and seared as quickly as a piece of beef." Instead, he recommends grilling his chops over coals on a medium hot grill "until the meat firms up [don't poke it with forks and such], flip it once with tongs [don't move it around more than twice per side for grill marks . . .] then let it rest for 5 minutes in the pan off the flame." I found that the chops needed just about 5 minutes on each side to "firm up." Following these directions, you will not fail. I love these chops served with a side of the Horseradish Cheese Grits with Confetti of Roasted Poblano Peppers and Red Onions (page 94).

2 (10- to 16-ounce) Caw Caw Creek (or another sustainable supplier's) pork chops
1 tablespoon olive oil
Salt and freshly ground pepper
1/4 cup farmers market hot pepper jelly
1 tablespoon water

Prepare coals in advance; light, then burn until the flame is at a medium-high heat, or until you can hold your hand close to the flame without scorching for a full 3 seconds. Rub down room-temperature pork chops with oil and season on both sides with salt and pepper. Cook according to Emile's directions, above. Remove from the grill and rest on a platter. Combine the pepper jelly and water in a small saucepan and blend together over medium heat. Brush down each chop on both sides with the pepper jelly. Continue resting the pork, covered with loosely fitted aluminum foil, for 15 minutes. Each chop is easily big enough for two, so cut each in half, horizontally, unless you're feeling really piggish. In which case, just serve them whole. Serve immediately.

Serves 4

SWEET ENDINGS

SPRING THROUGH EARLY SUMMER

Strawberry Mint Clafoutis 124

SUMMER

Baked Peaches with Red Wine Sorbet
    and Cream 126
Blues-Busting Blueberry Ice Cream 128
Stewed Plum, Globe Grape,
    and Peach Compote 130
Angel Food Cake with Muscadine and
    Strawberry Coulis Topped with
    Fresh Whipped Cream 131
Berry Coddled Cobbler 132

FALL

Perfectly Pumpkin Ice Cream 134
Plump 'n' Spicy Pumpkin Cookies 135
Baked Apples with an "Apple-y"
    Honey-Butter Sauce 136
Stuffed McIntosh Apple Crisps 137
Spicy Long Island Cheese Squash Soufflé
    with Warm Rum Cranberry Cream 138

YEAR-ROUND

Local Honey Cinnamon Ice Cream 141
Warm Wild Cherry Carolina
    Gold Rice Pudding 142

STRAWBERRY MINT CLAFOUTIS

Perhaps nothing better heralds the much-awaited arrival of spring than the first berry of the season: plump, juicy, regally red strawberries. In a good season (which is largely dependent upon a temperate fall), you'll be hard-pressed to make it home with a whole quart of them, since eating them out of the box is so hard to resist.

If you do, put them to use in a simple clafoutis, which is essentially a crêpe batter baked with whole fruit. Originally, the French country tart/pudding hailed from Limousin in central France and was prepared with whole cherries. The batter, however, lends itself to many fruits. The whole strawberries rise to the top and offer strands of juicy pinkness and tart sweetness throughout. If you're not a mint fan, skip it.

2 tablespoons flour

2 tablespoons sugar

2 eggs (preferably local)

1 cup whole cream

Pinch of salt

1 teaspoon vanilla extract

1 tablespoon chopped
   fresh mint

1 quart fresh whole
   strawberries, green tops
   removed and rinsed

Preheat oven to 350 degrees. In a mixing bowl, whisk together the flour and sugar. Form a well in the center and add the eggs, cream, salt, vanilla, and mint. Gradually incorporate into a smooth batter, whisking well. Generously butter a 9-inch pie pan. Line the bottom with whole strawberries, top-down. **NOTE:** Use enough to entirely fill the bottom—the quantity will depend on the size of the berries. Pour the batter over the top. Bake 40 to 50 minutes, or until the edges are nicely browned and the center is set.

If desired, brush the top of the warm- to room-temperature clafoutis down with a thin layer of warmed strawberry jelly for added sheen. Serve warm with a generous dollop of whipped cream, a fresh strawberry, and mint leaf for garnish.

Serves 6–8

STRAWBERRY STORAGE

Usually these gems don't hang around long, but if you find yourself with one berry too many, refrigerate market-fresh berries in the aerated paper packaging they come in. Don't wrap with plastic—they need air flow. Never wash strawberries until you're ready to use them, and do so with care. A quick rinse and a pat dry with a towel is all they need, if anything. Use them within 1 to 2 days of purchase. Tired strawberries are excellent candidates for an impromptu fruit salad or a puree to top ice cream, to make an instant sauce, or to utilize in the clafoutis recipe.

BAKED PEACHES
WITH RED WINE SORBET AND CREAM

Few things in life can beat the sheer indulgence of biting into a tree-ripened Southern peach while the juices run down your chin and the peach nectar kisses your soul. Indeed, a fresh, ripe peach is so succulent, like a strawberry, it seems practically aberrant to alter it in any way. In this dish, the peaches are briefly baked to soften them further and to make peeling the peaches easier. They are served with a cinnamon-spiked red wine sorbet and a bath of cool cream. The whole ensemble dresses up the peaches very nicely without altering their ambrosial essence.

FOR THE SORBET

2 1/2 cups full-bodied red wine,
  such as a Cabernet or
  Burgundy
1 stick cinnamon
2 whole cloves
1 sprig fresh mint
1 cup sugar
1 cup water

FOR THE PEACHES

6 peaches, ripe yet firm to
  the touch
1/2 cup whole cream
Fresh mint, to garnish

To prepare the sorbet, bring the wine, cinnamon, cloves, and mint to a boil in a saucepan over high heat. Reduce the heat to a low simmer and cook 10 minutes; set aside to cool. Separately, combine the sugar and water in a small saucepan. Bring to a boil for 30 seconds. Stir to dissolve the sugar; set aside to cool. Combine the wine and sugar water (or "simple syrup") in a bowl, straining the solids and discarding. Cool over ice or in the refrigerator. When very cold, freeze in an ice cream maker according to the manufacturer's directions. **NOTE:** If you don't yet own this handy kitchen accoutrement, place the sorbet in a container in the freezer and stir every 15 minutes to soften and smooth it as it freezes.

To prepare the peaches, preheat oven to 325 degrees. Trim the base of each peach to flatten it. Arrange peaches, evenly spaced, on a baking sheet. Bake until just softened, about 10 to 15 minutes; cool. Remove skins and pits, leaving peaches whole. Refrigerate, covered, for several hours or overnight until ready to use.

To serve, drizzle some cold cream on six individual plates or pretty, shallow bowls. Place the peaches in the center and fill each peach with a generous scoop of the sorbet. Garnish with fresh mint sprigs and serve immediately.

Serves 6

BLUES-BUSTING BLUEBERRY ICE CREAM

Blend and freeze four ingredients and, minutes later, you've got this creamy, frozen confection of plump, purple blueberries and cream. This egg-free version of ice cream demands the sweetest gems of summer for maximum flavor and color. Don't expect this to last too long. You'll be making your next batch before you know it. Rinse the berries just before using, no sooner.

2$^1/_2$ cups fresh blueberries, rinsed
1 cup sugar
Juice of 1 small lemon
3 cups whole cream

Puree the blueberries with the sugar and lemon juice in the bowl of a food processor until smooth. Pour into a large bowl. Whisk in the cream until thoroughly combined. Pour into an ice cream maker and freeze according to the manufacturer's directions. Serve in separate bowls garnished with a few fresh blueberries and a sprig of mint.

NOTE: This can also frozen in a container in the freezer and stirred every 15 minutes as described in the previous recipe.

Makes about 1$^1/_2$ quarts

STEWED PLUM, GLOBE GRAPE, AND PEACH COMPOTE

These colorful fruits thrive in Southern heat and burst onto the scene in tandem through the dog days of summer. Simmered together, the purple hues of the plums and grapes contrast with the orange/yellow colors of peaches, and the sweet and tart elements of each are bridged with some lovely local honey. Serve with a dollop of freshly whipped cream.

2 cups fresh plums, halved and
    pitted
2 cups fresh globe grapes,
    halved and seeded
2 medium-size fresh, ripe
    peaches, pitted and cut into
    1/2-inch-thick slices
Juice of 1/2 lemon
3 tablespoons local honey
Pinch of salt
1/4 cup water

In a large saucepan, combine all ingredients and bring to a boil over high heat. Reduce heat to medium-low and simmer 15 minutes, or until the fruit is softened; remove from the heat. Serve hot, at room temperature, or cold. The compote will store for several days in an air-tight container in the refrigerator.

Serves 6

ANGEL FOOD CAKE
WITH MUSCADINE AND STRAWBERRY COULIS TOPPED WITH FRESH WHIPPED CREAM

Muscadines are a thick and sour-skinned grape that is native to the Southeast. Though often put to use in jellies, ciders, and wines that are sold in myriad forms at Southern farmers markets, they are rarely eaten off the bunch like their sweeter-skinned grape cousins. Cooking the grapes slowly in a bit of water eventually peels the tough skins away from the fruit. Once the skins and seeds are discarded through a strainer, the remaining sweet grape flesh is quickly cooked with another warm-weather fruit such as strawberries, peaches, or raspberries to create a thick, gelatinous, fruity sauce (or coulis).

When paired with summer's best cake pal and whipped cream, the combination is unbeatable. And if you use a store-bought cake like me, this celestial dessert takes all of 15 minutes to prepare. Don't ever wimp out and buy prepared whipped cream, however! Making freshly whipped cream is as easy as pushing a prepared can's button and is free of emulsifiers, chemicals, and the unbearably noxious flavor of canned whipped cream.

FOR THE COULIS

4 cups red muscadine grapes, rinsed and stems removed

1/2 cup water

1 tablespoon wild local honey

3 tablespoons sugar

Juice of 1/2 lime

1 pint fresh strawberries, cleaned

FOR THE WHIPPED CREAM

1 pint whipping cream

3 tablespoons sugar

1 teaspoon good-quality vanilla extract

1 angel food cake

Mint sprigs and several fresh grapes, to garnish

To prepare the coulis, place the grapes, water, honey, sugar, and lime juice in a large saucepan; bring to a boil and reduce to a simmer. Cook until the skins have separated and the flesh of the grapes is soft, about 15 minutes. Meanwhile, remove the green tops of the strawberries and cut into slices; set aside. When the grapes are cooked, strain through a fine sieve and discard the solids. Return the strained sauce to the pan. Add the strawberries and cook over a low simmer until softened, about 5 minutes. Remove from the heat and set aside.

To prepare the whipped cream, pour the cream into a medium chilled metal or glass bowl. Add the sugar and vanilla. Whisking by hand or using an electric mixer, whip until firm peaks have formed. Cut the cake into eight 3- to 4-inch-thick wedges. To serve, spoon about 1/4 cup of the warm or room-temperature coulis into eight shallow bowls. Top each with a slice of cake and a generous dollop of whipped cream. Garnish with a sprig or two of fresh mint and a fresh grape.

Serves 8

BERRY CODDLED COBBLER

Just as blueberries are nearing the end of their season, blackberries and the South's justifiably renowned peaches start showing up at markets, making this the sweetest time of the year for fruit lovers. Besides eating these regally hued fruits out of the basket or over a sink while their juices dribble down your greedy chin, they're best put to use in a cobbler. Who doesn't love one? Easier than pie and just as delicious, a cobbler is welcome any day of the year.

This recipe employs cornmeal for added texture to what is otherwise a basic pie pastry, and for sweetness, farmers' market honey. Pair this with Local Honey Cinnamon Ice Cream (page 141) or creamery-fresh heavy cream.

FOR THE PASTRY:

1 1/4 cups all-purpose flour

1/4 cup yellow plain cornmeal

Generous pinch of salt

1 tablespoon sugar

6 tablespoons frozen butter, cut into rough 1/4-inch cubes

3 tablespoons frozen shortening, cut into rough 1/4-inch cubes

3 to 4 tablespoons ice cold water

FOR THE FILLING:

1 quart blackberries

1 quart blueberries

4 peaches, peeled and cut into coarse chunks

1/2 cup local honey

2 tablespoons cornstarch

Zest of 1 lemon

4 tablespoons butter

Preheat oven to 425 degrees. To make the pastry, pulse the flour, cornmeal, salt, and sugar together two or three times in the bowl of a food processor fitted with a plastic blade. Add the cold butter and shortening and pulse another eight or ten times, or until mixture looks like small peas. Drizzle the cold water through the mouth of the processor while pulsing until the pastry just starts holding together. Turn out the pastry onto a lightly floured surface and form into a 2-inch-thick disk. Wrap well in plastic wrap and refrigerate for at least 30 minutes. **NOTE:** The pastry can be made up to three days in advance and stored in the refrigerator, and it also keeps well in the freezer for up to three months.

Meanwhile, in a large bowl, toss together the berries, peaches, honey, cornstarch, and lemon zest until evenly coated. Once the pastry has rested, roll out to 1/4 inch thickness and drape it over a 2-quart pie dish, baking pan, or soufflé dish. (There should be some excess pastry hanging over the edges). Press the pastry into the pan and pour in the filling. Top the fruit evenly with pats of butter. Fold the excess pastry back over the fruit, tearing off any large pieces to top the fruit in the middle of the pan. Bake in the center of the oven until bubbling and golden brown, about 40 to 50 minutes. Serve warm.

Serves 8

PERFECTLY PUMPKIN ICE CREAM

It's probably been fifteen years since I last purchased a can of pureed pumpkin—sometime around the time I discovered the joy and simplicity of fresh roasted pumpkin. The added dimension of sweetness and deep, roasted color can't be found in any can and gives so much to this elegant and simple ice cream. Served atop a slice of holiday pumpkin pie or eaten by the spoonful from a bowl, this dish can't be beat.

1 pie pumpkin
1¼ cups whole milk
2 cups whipping cream
¾ cup granulated sugar
6 egg yolks (preferably local)
1 teaspoon vanilla extract
1 teaspoon pumpkin pie spice
1 teaspoon cinnamon
Pinch of cloves

Preheat the oven to 425 degrees. Cut the pumpkin in half, horizontally, scoop out and discard the seeds and any stringy flesh, and place both halves cut-side down on a baking sheet. Roast for 1 hour, or until the flesh is soft. Allow to cool, then peel off the skin and discard. Puree the flesh in a food processor until smooth. Reserve ¾ cup for this recipe. Any remaining puree can be refrigerated for several days or frozen for several months. Refrigerate until completely cold. **NOTE:** The puree can be made several days in advance.

Bring the milk and cream to an aggressive simmer over medium-high heat in a saucepan. Whisk together the sugar and egg yolks until frothy and lemon-colored. Whisk in the remaining ingredients, including the cooled, reserved pumpkin puree, until smooth. Once the milk and cream come to a simmer, slowly whisk them into the egg mixture, stirring constantly. Return the mixture to the saucepan and cook over medium heat, stirring constantly with a wooden spoon. The custard is done once it starts to coat the back of the spoon and the bubbles from the top have disappeared. Remove it from the heat and strain through a fine strainer into a bowl set into a bed of ice; let cool, stirring occasionally.

It's best to let the custard chill overnight, or for several hours, but it will work fine to freeze the custard once it's substantially chilled from its ice bath. Freeze in an ice cream maker according to the manufacturer's directions. Soften at room temperature for a few minutes before serving. This ice cream is excellent with good old-fashioned gingersnaps.

Makes 1 quart

PLUMP 'N' SPICY PUMPKIN COOKIES

These cake-like, chewy, soft cookies are perennial mainstays in my mother's kitchen. She's usually found preparing them as the weather cools and her thoughts turn to holiday gift bags and cozy afternoons wrapped up with these cookies, silence, and a cup of tea. Of course, unlike mom, I use freshly roasted pumpkin puree (you should have enough left over from the ice cream on previous page to make these cookies, by the way), but the rest of the recipe remains as she found it about twenty years ago in Southern Living *magazine.*

1 1/2 cups brown sugar

1/2 cup shortening

1 teaspoon vanilla extract

1 teaspoon lemon extract

2 eggs, well-beaten

1 1/2 cups fresh roasted pumpkin puree (see Perfectly Pumpkin Ice Cream recipe on previous page)

1/2 teaspoon salt

1/4 teaspoon ground ginger

1/2 teaspoon ground nutmeg

1/2 teaspoon ground cinnamon

2 1/2 cups all-purpose flour

4 teaspoons baking powder

1 cup chopped walnuts

Preheat oven to 350 degrees. In a large bowl, cream together the sugar and shortening until fluffy. Add the extracts, eggs, and roasted pumpkin. Beat together until smooth and light.

Sift together the salt, spices, flour, and baking powder. Using a wooden spoon, fold this mixture, in batches, into the blended wet ingredients until smooth. Fold in the walnuts and stir gently to combine.

Grease a cookie sheet lightly with shortening. Drop the dough by rounded teaspoons onto the sheet, evenly spaced. (Count on about 12 cookies per sheet). Bake until golden, about 15 to 20 minutes. Cool on a baking rack. Store in an airtight container until ready to serve. They will store well like this for up to 3 days, but after that, they start losing moisture and get a little tough.

Makes 4 dozen

BAKED APPLES
WITH AN "APPLE-Y" HONEY-BUTTER SAUCE

Select a firm, tart, sweet apple such as a Granny Smith or an heirloom variety such as Winesap for this sophisticated take on an old-fashioned classic. Though the apples are peeled, their skins are saved and simmered together with butter, honey, lemon juice, cinnamon, and a splash of apple brandy to come together into a pure essence of sweetened apple and butter decadence.

FOR THE APPLES

¼ cup unsalted butter

4 Granny Smith apples, washed, peeled, cored, and halved (reserve apple peels separately)

½ cup granulated sugar

½ cup Calvados (substitute Apple Jack brandy)

FOR THE SAUCE

½ cup wild honey

3 tablespoons butter

Juice of ½ lemon

½ teaspoon ground cinnamon

Reserved apple peels

Pinch of salt

½ cup cold unsalted butter, cut into ¼-inch cubes

½ cup whipping cream

Dash of Calvados (substitute Apple Jack brandy)

Preheat oven to 350 degrees. Melt the butter in an ovenproof sauté pan over medium heat. Add the apples and sauté briefly, tossing to coat in the butter. Remove from the heat. Arrange the apples in a single layer in the sauté pan, rounded sides up. Sprinkle with the sugar. Drizzle with the Calvados, cover with foil and bake until tender, about 20 to 30 minutes; set aside and keep covered.

In a medium saucepan, melt the honey, butter, lemon juice, and cinnamon together over medium heat. Add the reserved apple peels and sauté until softened, about 3 minutes. Add the salt and any cooking liquids from the reserved cooked apples. Continue to cook the sauce over medium-low heat until the peels have softened and the liquid has reduced to about ¼ cup. Spoon the sauce and peels into a fine strainer over another saucepan and press firmly with the back of a ladle to extract any pulp, juice, and flavor; discard the solids.

To finish, return the saucepan to the stove over high heat and bring the sauce to a simmer. Reduce heat to medium. Gradually whisk in the butter until it is frothy and incorporated. Add the cream and a dash of Calvados; heat through. Serve over the warm apples, lightly coating each with the warm sauce; serve immediately. Serve with freshly whipped cream or fresh vanilla ice cream for an extra special treat.

Serves 6–8

STUFFED MCINTOSH APPLE CRISPS

The quintessential comfort food, these stuffed, baked apples remind me of the simple delights of childhood and are more rustic and less involved than the preceding recipe. Try them as a variation on the never-gets-boring baked-apple theme. The soft flesh of the McIntosh apple starts to dimple and round with the crisp, buttery weight of the filling while it bakes. The contrast of the warm apple sitting in a shallow pool of cool, unsweetened cream is irresistible, pretty, and loved by all.

6 McIntosh apples

1 cup old-fashioned oatmeal

½ cup currants

1 cup finely chopped walnuts

½ cup light brown sugar

6 tablespoons unsalted butter, melted

1 tablespoon ground cinnamon

¼ teaspoon ground nutmeg

Pinch of cloves

Pinch of salt

1 teaspoon grated lemon zest

Whole cream

Preheat the oven to 325 degrees. Cut the top off each apple (about ¼-inch-thick) and set the tops aside. Using a soup spoon, core the apples, removing a bit of the flesh to create a ½-inch-thick shell around the perimeter of the apple; discard the cores. Arrange the apples in a small roasting pan, cored side up. (If the apples are wobbly on the bottom, trim their bottoms to flatten).

Combine all the remaining ingredients except the cream in a medium bowl, stirring well to combine. Fill each apple generously with this mixture, packing firmly. Top each apple with one of the reserved tops.

Bake until soft, about 45 minutes to 1 hour depending on the size of the apples. Serve hot out of the oven in a shallow bowl and drizzle with a few tablespoons of cool whole cream.

Serves 6

SPICY LONG ISLAND CHEESE SQUASH SOUFFLÉ
WITH WARM RUM CRANBERRY CREAM

Ladies, bring your beau or at least a sturdy basket to the market if you're thinking about toting home one of these hefty heirloom pumpkins, which weigh in at around 6 to 10 pounds. You'll find this winter squash will be worth the effort. When cooked, the bright orange flesh is fluffier than pumpkin and sweeter, too. Its background flavor is reminiscent of carrots. A lovely delight, it looks like a large, squashed round of cheese (hence its name) and has a gorgeous tan rind with sage green undertones.

Don't get put off by the lengthy directions in this recipe or the word "soufflé." It's really nothing more than a flavored classic white sauce (béchamel) and mounted egg whites. The keys to success are making sure that the béchamel is not too hot when the egg whites are folded in and that the egg whites are properly mounted. The béchamel can be prepared a day in advance and the egg whites can be mounted within 20 minutes of baking. It will cook while you relax, filling your house and your guests with all kinds of goodness and stomach-grumbling anticipation. And if it falls before its time, don't fret. It will still taste incredible and look great—just more like a pudding than a soufflé.

1 Long Island Cheese squash

FOR THE SAUCE

¼ cup dried cranberries
¼ cup dark rum
Butter
1½ cups whole cream
1 cinnamon stick
1 tablespoon vanilla extract
⅓ cup granulated sugar

Up to several days in advance, roast off the squash, keeping in mind that leftovers can be refrigerated and frozen for later use in soups, custards, etc.

Preheat the oven to 425 degrees. Cut the squash in half horizontally. Scoop out the seeds and discard. Place both halves cut side down on a baking sheet and roast until the squash has softened and collapsed, about 1 hour. Allow to cool. Scoop out the flesh and puree in a food processor until smooth; reserve ½ cup for use in this recipe.

On the day of service, begin with the prep for the cream sauce. Combine the cranberries and rum in a small glass bowl. Microwave on high for 1 to 2 minutes; set aside. Preheat the oven about 1 hour before you're going to bake the soufflé. Butter a large soufflé dish generously and rim with a 3-inch-high aluminum collar.

continued on page 140

FOR THE BÉCHAMEL

2 cups whole milk

1/2 tablespoon grated fresh
    gingerroot

1/2 teaspoon cinnamon

1/8 teaspoon ground cloves

1/8 teaspoon ground nutmeg

1 teaspoon vanilla extract

Generous pinch of salt

1/3 cup all-purpose flour

1/3 cup plus 2 tablespoons sugar

2 tablespoons unsalted butter,
    at room temperature

1/2 cup roasted Long Island
    Cheese squash, pureed

4 egg yolks

FOR THE MERINGUE

6 egg whites

Pinch of salt

1/2 cup sugar

Powdered sugar

To prepare the béchamel, bring the milk, ginger, cinnamon, cloves, nutmeg, vanilla, and salt to a boil and reduce to a simmer. In a small bowl, add a few tablespoons of cool water to the flour to make a loose paste. Gradually whisk flour mixture into the milk mixture. Reduce heat to medium. Stir until thickened, about 4 minutes. Remove from the heat and whisk in the sugar, butter, and roasted squash until smooth. While still warm, but not hot, whisk in the egg yolks, one by one, until incorporated; set aside.

In a very clean, large metal or glass bowl, beat the egg whites gently with a whisk until frothy. Add salt and, with an electric beater, beat on high until soft peaks form. Gradually add the sugar and continue to beat until firm peaks form. Whisk one-third of the meringue into the béchamel base. Delicately fold the second third into the mixture and repeat with the remaining meringue. Gently spoon mixture into the prepared soufflé dish. Place in the center of the oven on the lower rack. Turn heat to 375 degrees and bake for 50 to 60 minutes, or until firm but springy to the touch.

While it's baking, finish the sauce. Combine the soaked cranberries and rum with the remaining sauce ingredients in a small saucepan. Bring to a boil and reduce to a simmer. Cook until the liquid is reduced by half, about 30 minutes. Remove cinnamon stick and keep warm over low heat. When the soufflé is done, serve immediately sprinkled with powdered sugar. Spoon about 1/4 cup of the sauce over each serving.

Serves 8

LOCAL HONEY CINNAMON ICE CREAM

This Moroccan-esque combination of cinnamon and rich, local honey is simple and earthy. The ice cream reflects the amber tones of the honey and also goes fabulously well with Plump 'n' Spicy Pumpkin Cookies (page 135).

½ cup local honey

1 teaspoon vanilla extract

4 egg yolks

2 teaspoons ground cinnamon

3 cups whole cream

Whisk together all the ingredients except the cream in a medium bowl until frothy. Meanwhile, heat the cream over medium-high heat in a saucepan until simmering just below a boil. Gradually drizzle the hot cream into the mixture. Take it nice and slow so the cream doesn't cook the eggs. Return the mixture to the saucepan and cook over low heat, about 3 to 5 minutes, stirring constantly with a wooden spoon. Do not boil or the eggs will curdle. Once the foam on top has disappeared, the custard mixture is ready. Remove from the heat and chill in a bowl until cool. Freeze in an ice cream maker according to the manufacturer's directions, or use the stir and freeze method suggested for the other ice cream recipes in this chapter.

Makes 1 quart

WARM WILD CHERRY CAROLINA GOLD RICE PUDDING

Carolina Gold rice makes a sophisticated yet homey rice pudding when cooked low and slow in whole cream and fattened with rehydrated dried fruit (which is also readily available at regional farmers markets). In this recipe I use dried, tart cherries rehydrated with fresh pomegranate juice. The lemon and orange zest provide a pert, citrus finish. Serve warm, topped with pan-toasted, chopped Marcona almonds.

1½ cups whole cream

½ cup water

1 cup uncooked Carolina Gold rice

½ cup granulated sugar

1 fresh vanilla bean, cut in half lengthwise

Generous pinch of salt

½ cup lightly chopped dried tart cherries

¼ cup fresh pomegranate juice

Zest of 1 lemon

Zest from ½ orange

3 tablespoons half-and-half (as needed)

½ cup chopped Marcona almonds, toasted

In a medium saucepan, combine the cream, water, rice, sugar, vanilla bean, and salt. Bring to a boil and reduce to a gentle simmer. Cover and cook until the water and cream have been absorbed and the rice is tender, about 40 to 45 minutes.

Meanwhile, in a small bowl, combine the cherries with the pomegranate juice. Heat for 1 minute on high in the microwave and set aside.

When the rice is done, uncover and fluff gently with a fork. Remove the vanilla bean. With the edge of a paring knife, scrape the vanilla beans out of the pod and return to the rice, discarding the pod. Pour any remaining pomegranate juice from the cherries over the rice, lightly chop the cherries, and return them to the rice pot. Add the lemon and orange zests and gently fold all together. If the pudding seems too thick, fold in the additional half-and-half. Serve warm with almonds that have been toasted and coarsely chopped.

Serves 6

CAROLINA GOLD RICE

In the late-seventeenth century, a single bushel of golden, fragrant rice made its way into the thriving port of Charleston, South Carolina, via Madagascar. It's believed that the shipping merchant sold the rice to a plantation owner who successfully planted it; thus, the story of Lowcountry rice began. It is unlikely the merchant could foresee that this small transaction would morph into a whopping 200,000-plus acres of rice production and fuel 250 years of regional rice-based food traditions, from gumbo to Hoppin' John. Before the century was out, Charleston and the Carolina Lowcountry would explode with unprecedented, rice-born wealth.

After the abolition of slavery, large-scale rice production in the area came to a halt and was all but dead by the early 1900s. Yet the Lowcountry's love affair with rice, particularly Carolina Gold rice, never waned. By the late-twentieth century, in order to meet growing consumer demand, a number of small farmers in the region resurrected production of the revered grain. Today, Carolina Gold rice can be found in its signature cloth bag at farmers markets around the region, where it perfumes the air with its intoxicating nutty, buttery aroma.

STATE-BY-STATE SEASONAL PRODUCE CHARTS

The Southeastern region of the United States spans several hundred thousand square miles and includes a wide range of temperatures and terrains, from the flatlands and sub-tropic climes of Southern Florida to the cooler, mountainous terrains of the Piedmont region and Appalachian Mountains. Therefore, there are great variations in seasonal produce output, even within any given state.

With the aid of farmers market managers, markets, farmers, and Southeastern agricultural state websites, the following produce charts, arranged alphabetically and seasonally by state, have been provided to help you anticipate any given farmers market produce offerings at any given time, in any given state, throughout the respective growing seasons.

Please bear in mind that produce seasonality is dictated by Mother Nature, so if she's stingy with rain in April and heavy-handed with heat in August, there will be changes. The following are meant to give you a general idea of what to expect, but do not offer a 100 percent guarantee that what you're looking for will be there when you're looking for it.

ALABAMA

Apples	Mid-August through mid-October
Beans (Green, Snaps, etc.)	Mid-June through mid-September
Beets	Mid-May through mid-June
Blackberries	Mid-July through mid-August
Blueberries	Mid-June through mid-October
Broccoli	Mid-June through mid-July
Cabbage	Mid-May through mid-July, and mid-September through mid-October
Cantaloupes	June through August
Cauliflower	Mid-April through mid-June
Citrus	November
Corn	Mid-June through July
Cucumbers	June, and mid-September through mid-October
Eggplant	Mid-June through mid-September
Figs	August through mid-September
Grapes (Muscadines, Scuppernongs)	August through mid-October
Greens (Collards, Turnips, etc.)	Mid-February through July, and mid-September through December
Herbs	Mid-May through November
Lettuce	Mid-May through mid-October

Okra	June through mid-October
Onions	Mid-May through mid-October
Peaches	June through mid-August
Peas (Purple Hull, Crowders)	Mid-June through mid-October
Peas (Snow, English, etc.)	Mid-May through mid-October
Pecans	October through December
Peppers	Mid-June through mid-October
Persimmon	Mid-October through mid-December
Potatoes	June through mid-August
Potatoes (Sweet)	Mid-July through November
Pumpkins	October
Rutabaga	October and November
Spinach	Mid-April through mid-June
Squash (Summer)	Mid-May through mid-June
Squash (Winter)	Mid-September through mid-December
Strawberries	Mid-April through mid-June
Tomatoes	Mid-June through October
Watermelons	Mid-June through August

FLORIDA

Avocado	June through March
Bell Peppers	October through July
Blueberries	April through June
Broccoli	October through May
Cabbage	November through June
Cantaloupe	March through July
Carambala	August through March
Carrot	November through June
Cauliflower	November through May
Celery	November through June
Cucumbers	October through June
Eggplant	September through June
Grapefruit	September through June
Grapes	August through September
Guava	Year-round
Lettuce	November through May

Lime	Year-round
Longan	July through August
Lychee	June
Mango	May through September
Mushroom	Year-round
Onion	Year-round
Papaya	Year-round
Passion Fruit	July through March
Peanuts	May through December
Potatoes	January through July
Radish	October through June
Snap Beans	Year-round
Spinach	February through March
Squash (Summer)	September through June
Strawberries	October through June
Sweet Corn	August through June
Tangerines	September through May
Tomatoes	September through June
Watermelon	November through December, and April through July

GEORGIA

Apples	August through December
Arugula	April through June, and September through December
Asparagus	April through June and September through November
Bell Peppers	Mid-May through July
Beets	April through June and October through December
Blueberries	Mid-April through July
Broccoli	May through June and October through December
Brussels Sprouts	November through February
Cabbage	Early spring through winter
Carrots	December through June
Collards	October through June
Cucumbers	Mid-May through July, and mid-September through November
Eggplant	June through October
Field Peas	June through October

Figs	July through August
Grapes	Mid-June through October
Melons	May through July, and mid-September through October
Muscadines	Mid-July through October
Mushrooms	Year-round
Okra	May through October
Pecans	September through December
Peaches	Mid-May through mid-August
Radish	September through June
Snap Beans	April through June, and mid-September through mid-November
Strawberries	March through May
Sweet Corn	May through mid-October
Sweet Potatoes	September through November
Tomatoes	May through July, and mid-September through November
Turnips	October through April
Rutabaga	Fall through Winter
Vidalia Onions	April through November
Yellow Squash/Zucchini	Mid-April through mid-July, and mid-September through November

KENTUCKY

Apples	June through October
Asparagus	April through May
Beans (Green)	June through September
Beans (Lima and Pole)	July through September
Beets	June through October
Blackberries	July through August
Broccoli	May through June, and October through November
Chinese Cabbage	May through June, and September through November
Cantaloupe	July through September
Carrots	June through November
Cauliflower	May through June, and September through October

Cherries	June
Collards	May through June, and October through November
Corn (Sweet)	July through September
Cucumbers	June through September
Eggplant	July through September
Grapes	July through October
Kale	April through June, and September through December
Kohlrabi	June through July, and September through October
Lettuce	May through June, and September through October
Mustard Greens	April through June, and September through November
Onions (Bulb)	July through September
Onions (Green)	April through May
Peaches	July through August
Pears	September through October
Plums	August through September
Peas (Green)	April through May
Peppers	July through August
Potatoes	July through October
Raspberries	July through October
Radishes	April through May, and September through October
Strawberries	May
Tomatoes	July through October
Watermelon	July through August

MISSISSIPPI

Apples	Mid-May through mid-July
Beans (Butter)	June through September
Beans (Green)	Late April through mid-June, and mid-September through October
Beans (Pole)	Late April through mid-June, and mid-September through October
Blueberries	Mid-May through July
Broccoli	Mid-April through May, and October through December
Cabbage	April through May, and October through December

Cantaloupes	Early June through July
Cauliflower	Mid-April through May, and October through December
Corn (Sweet)	Mid-May through June
Cucumbers (Pickles and Slicers)	Late May through June
Eggplant	Mid-June through July
Greens (Collards, Mustard, Turnip, Kale)	Early March through early June, and October through November
Kohlrabi	April through mid-June
Muscadines	Early September through mid-October
Plums	Mid-May through July
Peas (English)	April through May
Peas (Southern)	Late June through August
Pecans	Year-round
Peppers (Bell, Hot)	Mid-June through July
Potatoes (Irish)	May through June
Potatoes (Sweet)	Year-round
Pumpkins	October
Squash (Winter)	October through November
Squash (Summer)	June through mid-October
Strawberries	Mid-May through July
Tomatoes (Field)	June through mid-August
Watermelons	Early June through July

NORTH CAROLINA

Apples	Mid-August through late February
Beans (Green)	Early June through late September
Beans (Butter)	Mid-July through August
Blueberries	Mid-May through mid-July
Broccoli	May and October
Cabbage	Early May through mid-December
Cantaloupes	July through August
Corn	Mid-June through mid-August
Cucumbers	June through mid-August
Eggplant	Mid-June through mid-August
Grapes	Mid-August through mid-October

Leafy Greens (Collards, Kale, etc.)	Mid-March through mid-December
Okra	Late July through August
Peaches	June through September
Peanuts	Year-round
Peas (Field)	July through August
Pecans	November through December
Peppers (Green)	Mid-June through mid-August
Potatoes	Mid-June through mid-August
Potatoes (Sweet)	Year-round
Pumpkin (Winter Squash)	August through October
Squash (Summer)	Mid-May through September
Strawberries	Mid-April through mid-June
Tomatoes	July through October
Watermelon	June through August

SOUTH CAROLINA

Asparagus	Mid-February through May, and early October through November (or first frost)
Beans (Lima and Butter)	June 1 through mid-October
Beans (Pole and Snap)	Mid-May through mid-July, and September through October
Beets	October through early June
Blackberries	Late May through mid-July
Blueberries	June through early August
Broccoli	Early November through mid-May
Cabbage	Early November through late May
Cantaloupes	Early June through mid-August
Carrots	Early October through mid-May
Corn	Early June through late August
Cucumbers	Early May through mid-July, and early September through mid-November
Eggplant	Mid-June through mid-October
Figs	Mid-July through mid-September
Greens (Collards, Kale, Mustard)	Early October through mid-June
Muscadines	Mid-July through early October
Okra	Early June through early October

Onions (Dry)	Early June through October
Onions (Sweet/Green)	Early January through late May
Peaches	Mid-May through late August
Peanuts (Green)	Mid-August through early November
Pears	Early August through early November
Peas (English)	Early February through early May
Peas (Field)	Early June through mid-October
Pecans	Mid-October through mid-December
Pepper (Sweet/Hot)	Early June through early October
Plums	Mid-June through mid-August
Potatoes (Fingerlings, Yukon Gold)	Mid-April through early August
Potatoes (Sweet)	Mid-August through early November
Radishes	Early October through mid-May
Rutabagas	Fall through Winter
Spinach (Mixed Salad Greens)	Early October through early June
Squash (Zucchini, Yellow)	Early May through early July, and early September through late November
Squash (Winter: Delicata, Buttercup)	Early September through late November
Strawberries	Mid-March through mid-June
Tomatoes	Early June through mid-July, and early October through late October
Turnips (Root Bunches and Greens)	Early October through early June
Watermelons	Early June through mid-August

TENNESSEE

Apples	Mid-June through December
Asparagus	Late April through May
Bok Choy	Early October through mid-November
Beets	July
Bell Peppers	Early July through early October
Blackberries	Early June through early October
Blueberries/Boysenberries	Late June through late August
Broccoli	May/June and October through mid-November
Cabbage	Early May through mid-November
Cantaloupe	Late June through early September
Cauliflower	Early May through early June

Chinese Cabbage	Early October through mid-November
Cherries	Mid-June through July
Carrots	Early May through early July
Collards	Early April through early June
Corn (Sweet)	Late June through late September
Cucumbers	Mid-June through September
Eggplant	Early July through September
English Peas/Field Peas	Early July through mid-October
Garlic	Mid-June through August
Gooseberries	Mid-June through July
Grapes	Late July through mid-September
Greens	Mid-April through late June, and late September through late November
Hot Peppers	Early July through late October
Irish Potatoes	Early July through early October
Kale	Early May through late June, and late September through mid-November
Leeks	Early June through late July
Lima Beans	Early July through mid-October
Muscadine Grapes	Late July through mid-September
Nectarines	July
Okra	Mid-July through early October
Onions	May through late August
Peaches	Early June through mid-September
Pears	Early September through early October
Pecans	October through December
Pole Beans/Shelly Beans/Snapbeans	Mid-June through September
Potatoes (Sweet)	Late August through March
Pumpkins (Winter Squash)	October through November
Raspberries	Mid-May through early October
Rhubarb	May through late June
Spinach	May through late June
Squash (Summer)	June through October
Strawberries	May through early June
Tomatoes	Mid-June through mid-October
Turnips	Early September through November
Watermelon	Early September through late November

STATE-BY-STATE FARMERS MARKET LISTINGS

Due to the rapid growth of farmers markets across any given state, the best way to stay current on where you can find them is by word of mouth, curious exploration, chance, or via individual state or community farmers market websites which provide locations, addresses, market manager contact information, hours, dates of operation, and, in some cases, directions.

In addition, the Agricultural Marketing Service (AMS) at the USDA maintains a relatively current (updated annually) listing of farmers markets across the country. They are easily accessed by state and city, as well. To access this information, go to: www.ams.usda.gov, click on "Farmers Market" and then click on "Farmers Market Search" to find a market near you.

Here is a list of farmers markets/agricultural websites that provide farmers market listings by state:

ALABAMA

www.fma.state.al.us/
Run by the Farmers Market Authority for the State of Alabama, this website provides detailed information about its mission, "U-pick" operators, farm/roadside stands, farmers markets, and more. Click on "Farmers Markets" for a listing of markets within the state.

FLORIDA

www.florida-agriculture.com
One of the most complete websites on statewide farmers markets I've come across, this site comes from the Florida Department of Agriculture and Consumer Services and includes a complete list of farmers markets by county and market name. It even provides websites for some markets. Click on

"Farmers Markets" to get the listings.

GEORGIA

www.agr.state.ga.us
Provides a list of state farmers markets, both seasonal and yearlong. Click on "Divisions" and then "State Farmers Markets." A directory of the markets appears. Each can be accessed individually for location, hours, etc.

www.georgiaorganics.org
Provides a list of independent, community farmers markets with an emphasis on organic or sustainable produce and goods. Click on "Local Food Guide" and scroll to the listing of farmers markets.

KENTUCKY

www.fruitstands.com
This website offers farmers market directories for every state. Just click on the state of interest and a listing of farmers markets and fruit stands for that state will come up.

MISSISSIPPI

www.mdac.state.ms.us
This site by the Mississippi Department of Agriculture provides general information about Mississippi farming initiatives but doesn't currently provide a list of Mississippi markets. For that, go to www. usda.gov and do a search for farmers markets for the state of Mississippi.

NORTH CAROLINA

www.ncfarmfresh.com

Provides a list of state-owned and community-based farmers markets. There is also a listing of roadside markets, "U-pick" farms, etc. Click on either of these on the home page and then conduct a search by the market or county name.

SOUTH CAROLINA

www.certifiedscgrown.com
Provides a list of state-owned and community-based farmers markets arranged alphabetically by county and city. Click on "Find SC Grown," then click on either "SC State Farmers Markets" or "SC Community-Based Markets."

TENNESSEE

www.fruitstands.com
This website lists farmers market directories for every state and includes the only complete listing I was able to find for Tennessee. Just click on the state of interest and the listing of farmers markets (and fruit stands) within that state comes up.

MARKETS VISITED/ REFERENCED IN THIS BOOK

For easy reference, I've included a list of the markets I visited while writing and researching this book. These are not necessarily markets I endorse over any other market, but markets that were open and accessible during the research period for this book. I encourage you to explore these farmers markets and farmers markets everywhere for food and fun.

Please remember that dates, times, and locations for all farmers markets are subject to change, and that nearly all markets are closed on major holidays (Christmas, Thanksgiving, and New Year's Day). Before planning a visit, it's a good idea to call ahead using the phone numbers provided to confirm hours, etc. websites are included whenever available.

ALABAMA

Decatur/Morgan Farmers Market
1st Avenue SE
Decatur, AL
(256) 773-6543
April through first week of November, Monday through Saturday, 6 a.m. to 6 p.m.

FLORIDA

Bay County Farmers Market
2230 East 15th Street at the
    Fairgrounds
Panama City, FL
(850) 769-2645
www.fl-ag.com
Open April through mid-August, Monday through Saturday, 8 a.m. to 2 p.m.

GEORGIA

Green Market for Piedmont Park
12th Street entrance to the park
Atlanta, GA
(404) 875-PARK
www.piedmontpark.org
May through December, Saturdays from 9 a.m. to 1 p.m.

Morningside Farmers Market
1393 North Highland Avenue
Atlanta, GA
(404) 313-5784
Open year-round, Saturdays, 8 a.m. to 11:30 a.m.

KENTUCKY

Bowling Green Farmers Market
1331 Richpond Road
Bowling Green, KY
(270) 781-4101
Open April through October, Tuesday and Saturday from 6 a.m. until sold out.

MISSISSIPPI

Charles R. Hegwood Biloxi
    Farmers Market
Under the I-10 overpass on
    Howard Avenue
Biloxi, MS
(228) 435-6296
First Tuesday in April through last Thursday before Christmas, Tuesdays and Thursdays from 6 a.m. to 4 p.m.

NORTH CAROLINA

Carrboro Farmers Market
301 West Main Street

Carrboro, NC
(919) 932-1641
www.carrborofarmersmarket.com
Open March through December,
7 a.m. to noon

Raleigh State Farmers Market
1201 Agriculture Street
Raleigh, NC
(919) 733-7417
www.ncdamarkets.org
Open year-round, Monday
through Saturday, 5 a.m.
to 6 p.m.

WNC (Asheville) Farmers Market
570 Brevard Road
Asheville, NC
(828) 253-1691
www.ncdamarkets.org
Open year-round. Daily: 8 a.m.
to 6 p.m. in summer and 8 a.m.
to 5 p.m. in winter.

SOUTH CAROLINA

All-Local Farmers Market
620-A Gervais Street (at Gervais
    & Vine Restaurant), 2nd
    Saturday of the month and
    2803 Rosewood Drive (the
    parking lot of Rosewood
    Market), 4th Saturday of the
    month
Columbia, SC
(803) 917-0794
www.thehavensc.com
Open year-round. Both
locations are open from 8 a.m.
to noon.

Beaufort Farmers Market
Heritage Park (off Ribaut Road)
Beaufort, SC
(843) 470-3655
www.clemson.edu/beaufort
Open April through October,
Saturdays from 8 a.m. to noon.

Charleston Farmers Market
Marion Square at the corner of
    King and Calhoun Streets
Charleston, SC
(843) 724-7309
www.charlestoncity.info
Open April through December,
Saturdays, 8 a.m. to 2 p.m.

Columbia State Farmers Market
1001 Bluff Road
Columbia, SC
(803) 737-4664
Open year-round: Monday
through Saturday, 6 a.m. to
9 p.m. and Sunday, 1 p.m. to
6 p.m.

Greenville State Farmers Market
1354 Rutherford Road
Greenville, SC
(864) 244-4023
www.scda.state.sc.us
Open year-round, Monday
through Saturday, 8 a.m. to
6 p.m.

Mount Pleasant Farmers Market
Coleman Boulevard & Simmons
    Street, Moultrie Middle
    School
Mount Pleasant, SC
(843) 884-8517
www.townofmountpleasant.com
Open April through October,
Tuesdays, 3 p.m. until dark

Pee Dee State Farmers Market
2513 West Lucas Street
Florence, SC
(843) 665-5154
www.pdfarmersmarket.sc.gov/
Open year-round, Monday
through Saturday, 8 a.m. to
6 p.m.

TENNESSEE

Centerville Farmers Market
Riverfront Park
Centerville, TN 37033
(931) 729-5224

Nashville Farmers Market
900 8th Avenue North
Nashville, TN 37208
(615) 880-2001
www.nashvillefarmersmarket.org
Open year-round, Monday
through Sunday, 8 a.m. to 6 p.m.

West Tennessee Farmers Market
91 New Market Street
Jackson, TN 38301
(731) 425-8308
Open May 5 through November
5, Monday through Saturday, 6
a.m. to 6 p.m.

ACKNOWLEDGMENTS

Without the commitment and labor of small, local farmers there would be no fresh-from-the-earth produce, none of the of edible delights these individuals bring to our tables. Without the efforts of communities, big and small, to support these farmers through encouraging direct purchases of their goods at farmers markets, we would not be able to shop these splendid venues and fill our bodies and souls with their collective goodness.

Therefore, my heartfelt gratitude is extended, first and foremost, to small farmers and the consumers and communities that support them across the South. It was a profound pleasure to meet, talk with, and learn from these agents of goodness as I traversed eight states. Thank you everyone for generously sharing your information, your magic, your joy, and your time.

This book would not have been possible without the unfailing support of my friend, Steve Dowdney. Steve helped me not only navigate the course to the right publisher, but also maintained an engaging and supportive spirit that helped breathe renewed life into my (at times frazzled) soul. He was there for me every mile of the 3,000 (and then some) we logged to get to the farmers markets. I'm sure he'll never forget my nervous-Nellie, spastic flinching as we inched our way through blinding fog in the mountains near Asheville, North Carolina, or exactly how many times I told him to slow down! Hopefully he remembers the many good times and laughs and delicious meals we had along the way. Thank you, Steve.

Of course, without a medium, there would be no message. Gibbs Smith graciously granted me the medium. Special thanks to Pete Wyrick and Christopher Robbins for believing in me and for enduring the smoky, grass-fed beef dinner that would eventually lead us all to this particular finish line. Thank you to everyone at Gibbs Smith, including my ultra-patient and talented editor, Melissa Barlow, who was involved with this project. It has been my pleasure working with you.

Photographer Rick McKee made photo shoots not only easy, but fun—so much fun that I don't even hold it against him that he doesn't like onions, one of my favorite food staples.

My gratitude is extended to Charleston's *Post & Courier* newspaper and The Evening Post Publishing Company for believing in my Market Whimsy vision so many years ago and for allowing me to reprint some of the recipes I created for the newspaper column in this book.

What would a world, life, or a book be without friends and family? I owe so much to a small handful of people I cherish. My mother and father, who taught me how to appreciate the fruits of the earth and the hard work that goes into making them, and anything worthwhile, grow. They chased this with liberal doses of love and the generous gift of a university education, which enabled me to eventually shape a career that I love. My ex-husband and good friend, Greg Herrick, gets credit for supporting my Le Cordon Bleu education, both emotionally and financially, and his mother, Dori, for being such a great cook, friend, and inspiration.

My quasi-sanity would almost certainly be at risk without the waves of laughter and strong foundation of friendship I find in my tennis team, The Chargers. "Hoi!" to you gals and to our sage and inspiring mentor/instructor, Fredrik.

Life on my quiet little street, in my kitchen, and on my porch would be vapid, indeed, without the supportive, easy amity and witty banter of my neighbors. All, especially Lucie and Leiza, have been sincerely kind to me, even though I am a Yankee, walk my dog most mornings in my bathrobe, and, because I wasn't born here, will never truly be a Charlestonian.

Finally, love to the most honest and receptive recipe testers ever, the best friends on the saddest, happiest, and everything-in-between days: my dog Tann Mann and his predecessor, Waco.

INDEX

Metric Conversion Chart

Liquid and Dry Measures

U.S.	Canadian	Australian
¼ teaspoon	1 mL	1 ml
½ teaspoon	2 mL	2 ml
1 teaspoon	5 mL	5 ml
1 tablespoon	15 mL	20 ml
¼ cup	50 mL	60 ml
⅓ cup	75 mL	80 ml
½ cup	125 mL	125 ml
⅔ cup	150 mL	170 ml
¾ cup	175 mL	190 ml
1 cup	250 mL	250 ml
1 quart	1 liter	1 litre

Temperature Conversion Chart

Fahrenheit	Celsius
250	120
275	140
300	150
325	160
350	180
375	190
400	200
425	220
450	230
475	240
500	260